CISTERCIAN FATHERS SERIES: NUMBER THREE

WILLIAM OF ST THIERRY

Volume One

ON CONTEMPLATING GOD

PRAYER

MEDITATIONS

CISTERCIAN FATHERS SERIES

CISTERCIAN FATHERS SERIES: NUMBER THREE

THE WORKS OF
WILLIAM OF ST THIERRY

Volume One

On Contemplating God

Prayer

Meditations

translated by
Sister Penelope, CSMV

CISTERCIAN PUBLICATIONS
Spencer, Massachusetts
1971

Ecclesiastical permission to publish this volume was received from
Bernard Flanagan, Bishop of Worcester, 9 December 1969

Library of Congress Catalog Card Number: 77-152478

Printed in the Republic of Ireland by
Cahill & Co. Limited, Parkgate Printing Works, Dublin

CONTENTS

v

ON CONTEMPLATING GOD

INTRODUCTION

WILLIAM OF THIERRY[1] was born at Liège. We know little of his family except that they belonged to the nobility. He left his native country to pursue his studies, probably at Laon. Later he abandoned the schools to take the monastic habit in the Abbey of St Nicasius of Rheims, then at the height of its fervor. In 1119 or 1120 he was elected abbot of St Thierry near Rheims.

William felt himself hemmed in by the demands of his office, the direction of his monks and the administration of his monastery. Yet to these he added the role of a zealous promoter in the renewal which was then stirring the abbeys of the whole area.

His call to be head of an important house and, perhaps still more, his commanding position among the other abbots of the region testify to the reputation he must have already enjoyed—a reputation that was well merited, if we may judge from his first writings. In

1. Dom J. M. Déchanet's *William of Saint-Thierry: The Man and His Work* (Cistercian Studies Series 10) is the best approach to William of St Thierry. For a more philosophical point of view, *Oeuvres Choisies de Guillaume de Saint-Thierry* (Paris: Aubier, 1944). These two works obviate reproducing a bibliography here; we shall confine ourselves to citing particular studies only in so far as they are necessary to our exposition. However, because of its special interest and its date, we must mention the thesis of Abbot André Adam: *Guillaume de Saint-Thierry, Sa Vie et Ses Oeuvres* (Bourg, 1923). A brief *Life: Vita Willelmi* or *Vita Antiqua* (Paris, B. N. Lat. ms. 11–782, ff 340f.) was published by A. Poncelet in the Mélanges Godefroid Kurth (vol. 1, Liège, 1908, p. 65).

3

them, William shows himself a profound thinker whose philosophical doctrine draws inspiration from contact with the Greek Fathers. The originality of his thought is not, however, in opposition to an extreme care for theological orthodoxy.

We are able to understand William's character and temperament from the very first years of his abbacy. His rather delicate constitution, prone to sickness, accommodates itself better to repose than to the concerns of business. His mind is exacting and deeply religious, inclining him toward complete solitude. Yet at the same time, he is headstrong, almost aggressive, in the realization of a very high ideal, an ideal he desires to communicate—rather to impose upon those around him. Essentially this ideal is Bernard. William wants to put Bernard everywhere. For his own part he wants to live at his side, but to this his friend would not consent. This leads to a crisis of several years' duration which ends in 1135, when William leaves St Thierry. He joins at Signy a large group of Cisterican monks coming from Igny, which in turn was a foundation established by Bernard near Rheims. There he remained until his death, 8 September, 1148, save for only one known absence. He went a short distance to visit the Carthusians of Mont-Dieu. His activity during these last years was divided between defense of the Catholic faith against rash innovators, and the exposition of spiritual doctrine for souls hungry for perfection.

This résumé of William's life will be dull indeed if we overlook the seething life that characterized the twelfth century. William knew this century; he formed a part of it in many ways. He bore his share of worldly concerns which, though not primary, were yet very constraining. His principal causes for worry lay in temporal administration, services of the feudal regime, difficulties with the house of Roucy and the Viscount of Trigny, insubordination of peasants and bourgeois disturbed by the communal movement.

The burden of these affairs was all the heavier, in that William's soul aspired to that calm and peace which allows a man to devote all his attention to God. This very need for liberty, for escape from an all too encroaching world, was so keenly felt by a great many that it had given rise, especially within the immediately preceding decades, to new forms of the monastic life. The Cistercian Order is but one of these manifestations, perhaps the most characteristic in the eyes of the old monks—the Black Monks. These when touched by the example of the new—White Monks—had no other solution than to pass over to Cîteaux or to change the life of their own monasteries in imitation of Cîteaux. It was a movement of transformation and adaptation, which was particularly active in what is now northern France.

William was the friend of Bernard. Other Benedictine abbots look upon him as the representative, the spokesman and staunch supporter of the Abbot of Clairvaux, a man whose spirit was shared by all seeking renewal but whose friendship was William's prized possession. With Bernard he exchanged letters which often touch on monastic affairs—the passage of Benedictines of the province of Rheims to the new Order, the beauty of the life of the White Monks, its modification so as to be utilized among the Black Monks. At the center of the controversy aroused by this monastic renewal was the celebrated *Apologia* of Bernard directed to William. All these efforts for renewal led the Benedictine abbots of the province to enter upon a very profitable series of meetings.

But monastic affairs were not the only ones that devolved upon abbots in the life of the twelfth-century Church. It can be said that no ecclesiastical question passed them by. What is more, abbots participated by right in synods and councils and they were in constant communication with the episcopate.

Heading the agenda of the councils of this period we find the problems arising from the new intellectual movements. It was the moment when the episcopal schools were resolutely turning toward philosophy, and seeking the explanation of things in the light of reason; but their scientific development was such that they had to contend with an imprecise terminology and notions as yet insufficiently clear. The question of universals was, perhaps, the most serious of all. This single question raised the sharpest theological repercussions. Precisely what are ideas? Is there a corresponding reality in beings? And if the response is applied to the enunciation of the mystery of the Holy Trinity, then what is signified by the distinction of the divine Persons: three gods, three real persons, three aspects of the divinity, three ways of speaking? How, then, must we view the mystery of the Incarnation? The name of Abelard, more than any other, evokes these major problems. William had been through the schools. He was a philosopher, and yet more than anyone else he showed his concern for orthodoxy. He worried about these questions and eventually intervened, for his was never a temperament that could remain silent when aroused.

Temporal and secular business, ecclesiastical and theological affairs continually occupied William's attention and made him come out of himself, even when he desired to concentrate on but a single problem—knowing God in perfect love. For all that, he nevertheless succeeded in completing a magnificent spiritual itinerary revealed to us by his works.

Spiritual itinerary

It cannot be doubted that William's vocation was to live for God. This vocation led him to leave his home at Liège, and he seems never to have returned. We know nothing of his family. He attended the most renowned schools of the time in order to learn from the finest masters the science that leads to a knowledge of God. But he soon saw the perils of the academic milieu. More than the loose living of certain students, it was the excesses and pride of a science which speaks about God without being able to give him, that frightened William to the point where he sought another, safer school—the school of the Lord's service. He entered a monastery. Thus blessed with excellent intellectual and also spiritual preparation, he went on to develop the latter while not neglecting the former.

His outpourings, scattered here and there, or brought together in the collection of *Meditations*, reveal to us the secret of his prayer. For him, the problem was always one of apprehending the invisible God. This problem presents a double aspect, theoretical and practical.

The practical question lies in finding a way of life where the line of conduct determined by the theoretical principles can be most perfectly realized. This can be nothing other than solitude, a "desert," reproducing that Egypt where true monks once lived, the solitaries of the Golden Age. But where? More or less clearly we see William's aspirations trained on various particularly fervent centers: the canonical life of Mont-Notre-Dame or the monastic life at St Nicasius, the black habit of St Thierry or the white habit of Clairvaux, the Cistercian solitude of Signy or the Carthusian retreat of Mont-Dieu. Wherever it may be, he is destined to remain dissatisfied, for the true "sabbath" is only to be found in the repose of the celestial homeland.

The theoretical problem is one of rapport between knowledge and love. William was much too intellectual not to situate the possession of God in an act of contemplation, of knowledge. At the same time he was too practical not to take into account two other realities. On the one hand, all earthly knowledge takes its departure from sensible objects and from the concepts we form of them. Now God is spirit, transcendent being. Since he far surpasses the intelligence, it is necessary to compensate for its deficiency. On the other hand, in man who forms a complete whole, the act of the intellect is accompanied by an act of the will. The same holds true of God in the mystery of the Blessed Trinity. In both cases it is fitting to give place to love so as to realize, with the help of grace, a genuine connaturalness with God—to be one with him.

These principles are set forth in *On Contemplating God*, William's first treatise. But the ideas in it are still not too clear. They need to be specified, sounded. William here studied love, this divine faculty placed in us at creation, thrown off course by sin, restored by the sacrifice of Calvary. Love is essentially the union of the will with God, a union established by the Creator but which, from the very fact of our liberty, is capable either of being lost or of growing in an ascent that leads to the very plenitude of love, even to wisdom and to beatitude.[2]

2. *De Contemplando Deo:* PL 184:365–379. Of the same period and on the same subject: *The Nature and Dignity of Love* (*De Natura et Dignitate Amoris:* PL 184:380–408). Cf. M. Davy, *Guillaume de Saint-Thierry, Deux Traités de l'Amour de Dieu*. A translation will appear in Cistercian Fathers Series 15.

In order to realize this ascent more surely, a man must know himself, body and soul. William, therefore, undertook to study what he calls the "physique" of the body and the soul or, if one prefers, psychology.[3]

Then it is that he felt qualified to put into practice the theory of love which he had already studied. One book is to serve as his guide, *The Song of Songs*, the classic work on the subject. But still not daring to solo, he follows in the wake of his masters, Ambrose and Gregory—and also Bernard, with whom he confers during the course of an illness that immoblizes both of them at Clairvaux. These conversations only whet his desire to reside with Bernard in the wonderful solitude of the holy valley, living the words of the *Song*.[4]

Other demands, however, kept him at St Thierry. And other questions presented themselves, particularly that of grace. After having studied love and its subjects, he turned to the very source of love to scrutinize this great mystery. In what way does God give us his love and how do we receive it? Again in this area he followed in the footsteps of the masters—Paul, especially as explained by Augustine, Ambrose, Origen and others.[5] He also consulted Bernard who drafted a little exposition of the problem for him.[6] He did not stray from the constant object of his interest when he went on to write a book on *The Sacrament of the Altar*, the mystery

---

3. *De Natura Corporis et Animae:* PL 180:695–726. A translation of this treatise will appear in Cistercian Fathers Series 24: *Treatises on the Soul.*

4. *Excerpta ex Libris Sancti Gregorii Papae Super Cantica Canticorum:* PL 180: 441–474. *Commentarius in Cantica Canticorum e Scriptis Sancti Ambrosii:* PL 15: 1947–2060. Efforts are being made to ascertain whether elements of the Clairvaux conversations have come down to us in the *Brevis Commentatio ex Sancti Bernardi Sermonibus Contexta, Ubi de Triplici Statu Amoris:* PL 184:407–436. In our opinion, it is rather a question of a composite work reflecting the conversations of the two abbots. Cf.: Dom J. Hourlier, "Guillaume de Saint-Thierry et la 'Brevis Commentatio in Cantica' " in *Analecta Sacri Ordinis Cisterciensis,* XII (1956), pp. 105–114.

5. *Expositio in Epistolam ad Romanos:* PL 180:547–694.

6. St Bernard, *On Grace and Free Will* (*De Gratia et Libero Arbitrio:* PL 182:1001–1029); trans. D. O'Donovan, *The Works of Bernard of Clairvaux,* vol. 7 (Cistercian Fathers Series 19).

of the creature's encounter with the living God.[7] It would seem that William was now able to enter the "arcana of the Most-High," to explore that land of happiness where one enjoys the blessedness of complete love. He knew the nature of love and its development; he knew the man who loves; he knew the God who gives love and who is loved. Under the tutorship of the masters he had already scrutinized the mysteries of the book of ineffable love, the *Song*.

At Signy he made good use of his leisure. In deep seclusion, surrounded by "fields and beech trees," in what he considered full spiritual maturity, he undertook his personal commentary of the *Song*.[8]

Was he finally going to touch the summits? Not yet. A last purification awaited him. It is not that he was too subject to his sensibilities. Many saints, before the end of their lives, pass through a phase in which their faith is strengthened. Not necessarily a trial, it always issues in a more profound certitude and a greater knowledge, despite the obscurity of faith. It is entrance into a luminous cloud. For William, theological controversies furnished the occasion for this final phase. He left to Geoffrey de Lèves and to Bernard of Clairvaux the mission of entering the lists.[9] He nonetheless made his contribution to orthodoxy by composing treatises that will serve to confirm souls in faith. How could he fail to be the first to benefit from these?[10] There remained to him only one task—a synthesis of his doctrine and his experiences. He thus went on to draft his wonderful *Treatise On the Solitary Life*, dedicated to the

---

7. *De Sacramento Altaris:* PL 180:345–366.

8. *Expositio Altera Super Cantica Canticorum:* PL 180:473–546; trans. C. Hart, *The Works of William of St Thierry*, vol. 2, Cistercian Fathers Series 6.

9. See his letter to Geoffrey de Lèves and to St Bernard on the errors of Abelard: PL 182:531–533 and his letter to St Bernard on the errors of William of Conches: PL 180:333ff. See also, his *Disputatio Adversus Petrum Aboelardum:* PL 180:345–366.

10. *Speculum Fidei:* PL 180:365–397. *Ænigma Fidei:* PL 180:398–440. To these, we must necessarily add the *Sententiae Fidei*, now lost. A translation of the first two treatises will appear in vol. 3 of *The Works of William of St Thierry*, Cistercian Fathers Series 9.

Carthusians of Mont-Dieu, which became known to history as *The Golden Epistle*.[11]

Finally a duty of fraternal charity allows him to end his days with his friend, not by settling at Clairvaux, but by undertaking the *Life of Bernard*. The saintly abbot had no need of *The Golden Epistle*—he who was a master. William, therefore, owed him something else, something in which he intended only Bernard to be reflected. And yet, did not William more than once sketch his own portrait while painting that of his friend? Friendship makes two persons one; it holds all things in common.[12]

In the course of his work of fraternal love, William of St Thierry entered into his repose, "the perpetual sabbath," where perfectly and eternally "one sees him whom one loves, loves him whom one sees."

HISTORY OF THE TEXT

Ordinarily, *On Contemplating God* is placed at the beginning of William's abbacy. Dom J. M. Déchanet dates it at 1119 or 1120 although the draft, he says, may go back to the years at St Nicasius.[13] It is well to justify this date. We shall then see how the treatise has been preserved for us.

11. *Epistola seu Tractatus ad Fratres de Monte-Dei:* PL 184:307–354. The third book is not a part of William's work. The actual title is: *Epistola ad Fratres de Monte Dei.* Accompanying the treatise is a dedicatory letter. An English translation will appear in Cistercian Fathers Series 12, *The Works of William of St Thierry*, vol. 4. Dom Déchanet has published studies on it in "Un Recueil. Singulier d'Opscules de Guillaume de St-Thierry: Charleville 114," *Scriptorium*, VI, 2 (1952), pp. 196–212; VIII, 2 (1954), pp. 236–271; XI, 1 (1957), pp. 63–86. See too: "St Bernard Postulant Chartreux" in *Collectanea O.C.R.*, XV (1953), pp. 32–45; "Seneca Noster: Des Lettres de Lucilius à la Lettre aux Fréres du Mont-Dieu" in the *Mélanges Joseph de Ghellinck*, sj, Museum Lessianum, historical section no. 14, pp. 753–766 (Gembloux: Duculot, 1951). Other works on this subject are mentioned in *Oeuvres Choisies*, p. 48. To them we might also add: "Autour d'une Querelle Fameuse, de l'Apologie à la Lettre d'Or" in *Revue d'Ascétique et de Mystique*, XX (1939), pp. 1–34.

12. *Vita Bernardi, Liber I:* PL 185:225–268.

13. Dom J. M. Déchanet, *William of St-Thierry: The Man and His Works;* *Oeuvres Choisies*, p. 39.

Date

Toward the end of his life, William himself left a list of his works, when he offered them to the Carthusians of Mont-Dieu. This would be around 1145. His list is divided into two series—personal works, then anthologies. The historical clues found elsewhere show that each series follows a chronological order. By way of exception, the *Mirror* and the *Enigma* are placed at the top because of their current interest; the treatise, *On the Nature of Body and Soul*, is listed at the end. *On Contemplating God* figures at the beginning of the first list. Quite naturally then it can be concluded that this work was written at the outset of its author's career. Other lists add nothing more; either they are derived from the *Letter to the Carthusians* or their ordering seems to have been purely fortuitous.[14]

The manuscript tradition is only a relative help to us due to the fact that it does not give the works of William gathered into one corpus, but scattered, grouping them only by twos and threes. It merely guarantees the anteriority of *On Contemplating God* to the treatise, *On the Nature and Dignity of Love*.[15] Noteworthy, however,

14. A Passion-homilarium of St Thierry, Rheims 1407 (K 787), has a note on the first page dated June 11, 1402, enumerating William's works. The list is followed by the text of the *Letter*. The *Bibliotheca Ecclesiastica* (Hamburg, 1713), composed and annotated by Aubert Le Mire, and afterwards by J. A. Fabricius, allows us to follow what might be called William's reputation. Toward the end of the thirteenth century the pseudo Henry of Ghent mentions the *Treatise on the Solitary Life* and the *Life of St Bernard*. The editor adds the *Meditations*, according to the editions of Anvers. In the appendix, the *Commentary on Romans* is specified. In 1492, Trithemius came up with the almost complete list in the order found in the *Letter to the Carthusians*, except for two misplacements. The very different order of the *Vita Willelmi* offers nothing in the way of chronology. Perhaps it is founded on a somewhat loose logical basis. Dom A. Wilmart, "La Série et la date des ouvrages de Guillaume de St-Thierry," *Revue Mabillon*, 14 (1924), p. 157, thinks it was the order in which the books were arranged in the Signy library.

15. Whenever a manuscript contains both the *De Contemplando* and the *De Natura* they are connected, with *De Contemplando* coming first. This disposition may have arisen from the logical need to place a shorter, more affective, more prolix text as a preface to a more methodical treatise. The idea of anteriority, deduced from the *Letter*, is not excluded, its logic being found in the progress of the author's thinking.

are two very interesting manuscripts, contemporary with William, which contain more than the others. One that is especially valuable contains the works written at Signy, while the other reflects the period when William was at St Thierry. *On Contemplating God* is found in the latter and not in the former.[16]

The treatise itself seems to suggest the date 1119–1120. Along with a few others, it can be assigned to the period when William was already in charge of a monastery, since it indicates his concern for the brothers. If he leaves them for an instant, "about half an hour," he must not abandon them completely. He has not yet decided to pass over to Clairvaux, he has yet to ask Bernard to accept him. This request can be dated probably in 1124. In *On Contemplating God* William speaks of his monks. Manifest is the affective and intimate character of the exposition, which often gives it the appearance of a private meditation. However, the charm of the style creates the impression of an oral commentary in which the tone of voice, and nuances of the spoken word would make difficult sentences understandable. In many passages, the sequence of ideas, the turns of phrase, and the expressions are better understood if spoken. The punctuation of the manuscripts reveals a discourse in which the thought is protracted and recurrent. Sentences are suddenly broken off in order to accentuate what follows. The beginning seems indeed to be an invitation addressed to an audience. "Come, let us go up to the mountain of the Lord." Shall we some-day establish that these words have preserved for us the first instructions given by William to the monks of St Thierry? We would then conclude that he was opening himself to them, telling them what he had most at heart, his desire to see God—a desire he was then obligated to make them share.

It is also worthy of note that the *Song of Songs* is not cited in this

16. The works of Signy are contained in Charleville 114 where we find: *Treatise on the Solitary Life*, *Mirror of Faith*, *Meditations*, *Enigma*, and the personal *Commentary on the Song*. The works of St Thierry found in Mazarine 776 include: a fragment of the *Meditations*, the *Treatise on Contemplation*, *Treatise on the Nature and Dignity of Love*, *Prayer*, and other spiritual writings that are not William's. These two manuscripts do not give all of the works of William.

work into which it would fit so naturally. This carries us back to the time when William has not yet entered into the spiritual meaning of this book. Thus this work is prior to the time at Clairvaux when he and Bernard, both ill, would grapple with the significance of the *Song* together. The date of these conversations is not easy to determine, but we cannot set it any later than 1124.[17]

One last consideration seems decisive in establishing the date of *On Contemplating God* at the very beginning of William's abbacy. Even though, by the light of later writings, we recognize in this treatise the author's fundamental ideas, they are still imperfectly formed and expressed far less clearly than they will be in subsequent works. William's entire literary endeavor will be directed to making them more precise.

Dissemination

An inventory, even incomplete, of the manuscripts of *On Contemplating God* shows that, from century to century, the treatise has been copied to some extent in all the countries of the Latin Church.[18] The basic agreement of recent manuscripts shows that the dissemination stems from one copy. Only the preamble *In Lacu* of the Mabillon edition would cause any difficulty if it actually pertained to the text. But there is no such difficulty. *In Lacu* was a mistake on the part of the editor.[19] Collating proves that the whole

---

17. This dating is accepted by Dom J. M. Déchanet, *William of St Thierry.*

18. Many catalogs do not give the opening words and the pertinent remarks do not allow us to see, beneath the various titles, whether we are dealing with our treatise or not. This is the case with Munich, col. 3238 *Bernardi ab. Soliloquium*, 7745 *De Contemplatione*, 7791 *De Meditationibus, de Cognitione et de Dilectione Dei*, 8982 *De Contemplatione*, 9556 *De Amando Deo.*

19. *In Lacu* is a distinct work found in some manuscripts. One of them, that of the Dunes (Bruges 128), was the cause of Mabillon's mistake as well as of those who followed his edition. Cf. Dom J.M. Déchanet, "Le Pseudo-Prologue du *De Contemplando*" in *Cîteaux in de Nederlanden* 8 (1957). As regards both substance and style, it excludes all connection with William. We have thought it unnecessary to reproduce this pseudo-prologue in the present edition, as also a reading in the second section that is certainly unauthentic although it appears in certain editions.

tradition is derived from a single original. Contrary to what can be established for other works of William, this treatise does not show two successive stages in the text; the copies are distinguishable simply by their greater or lesser fidelity. In a general way, the nuances in his thinking, the ingenuity of his style, the word order, are lost all the more easily as the scribes, misled by the peculiarities of their period and still more so by a subtle author, tend to substitute their own mentality for that of William. Also noticeable is the fact that several copyists modify the text, apparently because they are thinking in French. A few share added mistakes properly so called— mistakes either in reading or in transcription. Thus we witness the corruption, more or less rapid, of a very personal text.

Written at St Thierry, *On Contemplating God* was probably kept in the library of this monastery, and perhaps of a few other houses such as St Nicasius or St Remy, for among these were frequent exchanges. We have good reasons for thinking that Bernard received a copy. His own treatise, *On Loving God*, would seem to be a reply to his friend.[20] The letter to the Carthusians proves that the treatise was to be found at Signy. It can readily be supposed that it was also copied at Mont-Dieu. Finally, when inviting his Carthusian friends to read it, William declares that they are not the first to do so.

But the library of St Nicasius is now almost wholly dispersed, while the one at St Remy was destroyed in the fire of 1774. What remains of it does not contain *On Contemplating God*. Should we then suppose that the author kept his treatise in autograph manuscript, lent it to Bernard, carried it with him to Signy, entrusted it to the Carthusians, who destroyed it? This can hardly be admitted in the face of so great a number of manuscripts of such varying ages and origins.

The dissemination of *On Contemplating God* thus raises a problem. We shall not arrive at the explanation except by dealing with still another question, that of ascertaining why the name of William, as an author, vanished so quickly. Almost all his writings remained

---

20. Cf. Dom J. Hourlier, "Saint Bernard et Guillaume de Saint-Thierry dans le 'Liber de Amore' " in *Analecta S.O.C.*, IX (1953), pp. 223–233.

anonymous or were hidden beneath the name of a third party. To our knowledge, only one manuscript presented *On Contemplating God* with an explicit indication of its true author. It is a beautiful manuscript of the twelfth century preserved today in the Mazarine Library after having passed through the monasteries of Reuil in Brie and of Martin-des-Champs. But until additional information is forthcoming, we must, unfortunately, resign ourselves to ignorance as to the origin of this volume so closely linked to one of the abbeys where William lived. This unusual attribution of the treatises to their real author is our surety.[21]

Less than fifty years after its redaction, *On Contemplating God* went under the name of Bernard. We find this, around 1165, on a manuscript from Anchin. The treatise, followed by *On the Nature and Dignity of Love*, comes after the *On Loving God* of Bernard, thus forming the second part of a trilogy. The work of Bernard here

---

21. Mazarine Library, ms. 776: cf. Augusto Molinier, "Catalogue des Manuscrits . . . de la Bibliothéque Mazarine," vol. I, Paris, 1885. He indicates that the volume comes from St-Martin-des-Champs where its old marking was 135. The manuscript does not figure on a list of the books of this monastery from the beginning of the thirteenth century: cf. Léopold Deisle, *Cabinet des Manuscrits de la Bibliothéque Nationale*, II, 235. Unless this catalog be incomplete, the manuscript does not come from the St-Martin scriptorium. On the other hand, it is hard to think that Dom Martin Marrier would have found it at Chaalis or at St-Arnoul de Crépy, during the second quarter of the seventeenth century because then it would have remained in the St-Martin Library in process of reconstruction. But in 1636 we find it inscribed in the Reuil catalog. Either it is something recently acquired or some careful librarian of the time is merely classifying his collection of ancient works as was done by many of his contemporary confrères. The manuscript bears three markings: 925 crossed out in black, 575 crossed out in red, 776 written in red. Not one of these markings antedates the seventeenth century and the last two have to do with the Mazarine Library. The first one would be a St-Martin marking: at Reuil it would presuppose a great many volumes in this little priory. It is not known by what sign Molinier was able to recognize in this manuscript the ancient 135 of St-Martin. We know of four other manuscripts of Reuil at Paris: Arsenal 260 (480 T.L.), Isidore, eleventh century; ib. 773 (28 J.L.), Augustine, Cassiodorus, twelfth century; Mazarine 678 (886), Gregory, etc. twelfth century; the National Library, lat. 17458, Hugh of St-Victor, twelfth century. Not one of them permits us to affirm that a copy of the *De Contemplando* was made at Reuil. Furthermore, the writing does not seem to be that of the manuscripts of St Thierry or of Signy of William's time.

bears the title *On Delight in God*; both of William's bear the heading *On Love*. And all three are attributed to the same author.[22] The course of manuscript tradition serves only to confirm what we have already noticed in the Anchin manuscript—*On Contemplating God* is ascribed to Bernard, its title is changed and it is incorporated into a whole with other writings.

Attribution to Bernard

Whether it is a question of this treatise or others it must be admitted that the Abbot of St Thierry never bothered to disseminate his works, and no one dared to shoulder this task for him. Certainly we see him putting the complete collection of his works into the hands of the Carthusians of Mont-Dieu, but the very terms in which he couches his consignment are extremely revealing. He does, indeed, like to show his writings to a few friends, to the initiate, we might call them; but he does so cautiously. He would rather see his manuscripts destroyed than in the possession of the contentious.

We can recognize here something other than timidity. There is a spiritual current in twelfth-century thought which drinks constantly from Greek sources, provoking the mistrust of many and the calumny of some. William is the best representative of this current, perhaps the initiator. By not naming his sources, or by presenting them in some vague way, he does his utmost not to shock. He utilizes more than he quotes. He assimilates the thought and transforms it into his own. His doctrine follows a well-beaten path, yet he remains fearful, or merely prudent. To the Carthusians he speaks of tracts composed for the use of the brothers, writings which might profit a sincerely religious soul. The limited dissemination indicates clearly that they hardly went beyond a rather restricted circle. Should we not conclude that William of St Thierry wrote and spoke only for his sons of St Thierry, his brothers of Signy, his

22. Douai ms. 372, vol. I. Cf. Dom J. Leclercq, "Études sur St Bernard et le Texte de ses Écrits," *Analecta S.O.C.*, (1953), pp. 124–136: "La Plus Ancienne Collection d'Oeuvres Complètes de St Bernard, le Manuscrit de Douai 372."

friends of Mont-Dieu? He did not want his works to have a wide circulation—perhaps out of prudence but more from a reluctance to cause disquietude.

This attitude, in conformity with William's character and temperament, points to his need for quiet, solitude and repose. As ardent as anyone, he is rather a thinker than a fighter. He seeks the truth in the fullness of its light. As much as he wants to share this, he does not try to impose it unless the matter touches essential principles. Even then, he pushes others—men of action—into the arena, reserving for himself the task of giving the warning and lighting the way.

It is Clairvaux that brought fame to William's writings a few years after the death of Bernard. We can easily see how this happened. The renown of Bernard provoked the multiplication of his works. Everywhere copies were made, not only of what was in circulation during his lifetime—not only of the authentic works—but of everything with a Bernardine flavor that could be found. Clairvaux surely possessed William's writings. Bernard, the unique friend, was indeed the first to whom the works of "his other self" were submitted, and we have proof of literary exchanges between them. Eager to have everything that was Bernard, the copyists seized upon all they found, building an immense file in which the apocryphal figured more and more. They did not bother to consider anything carefully; a slight resemblance sufficed.[23] From the beginning, confusion was easy, as the copies coming from St Thierry and Signy, or made at Clairvaux from the autographs, did not necessarily bear William's name.[24] We can thus understand how some manuscripts are anonymous while others pass under the name of Bernard.

There must have been among the first copyists, however, those who knew the real author, for the name of Bernard seems at times

---

23. *Venam imitantur et sanctimoniam redolent* says the 1520 Lyon edition of Bernard. The very title of the Tiraqueau edition tells us of the "supposed works, although of a similar piety." *Supposita quamquam non dissimilis pietatis.*

24. In many manuscripts, either the title or the name of the author was added by a later hand which often found very little space at its disposal.

to have been written over a scratched-out place in the parchment. These erasures prove the force of common opinion.

The printing press confirmed the position taken by the manuscripts. It would seem that the only exceptions were the *Meditations* and *On Contemplating God*, which the *Magna Bibliotheca Patrum* (1618), and its successor, the *Maxima Bibliotheca* (Vol. 22: 1677), ascribed to their true author. Though Bertrand Tissier published the majority of William's works under his name, it is in Vol. IV of his *Bibliotheca Patrum Cisterciensium* (1669) that they are to be found among the *Opera Omnia* of Bernard. In this he followed the general practice of keeping the Abbot of St Thierry in the slip-stream of the Abbot of Clairvaux. Thus William continued posthumously to realize the dream of his life—*subumbra illius quem desideraveram sedi*. With very rare exceptions, it was necessary to wait until the beginning of the twentieth century for the works of William to be presented apart from the Bernardine corpus, and until the middle of the century for the two treatises on love to be so separated.[25]

It remains to be explained how, among all of the writings of William, only certain ones have enjoyed extensive dissemination while the others have fallen into oblivion. Very few letters have been preserved for us. This is the common fate of this type of writing, except for a few particularly important collections, such as the correspondence of Bernard. One is, therefore, not astonished at the meagre returns afforded by this collection.[26]

---

25. Migne, PL 180, gives many of William's works to which must be added PL 15 for the commentary drawn from Ambrose. The rest, particularly the treatise, *On Contemplating God*, are found in the volumes devoted to Bernard, PL 182–185.

26. William's letters: to Rupert of Tuy (Deutz), c. 1126 (PL 180:341), to St Bernard, 1128 (*ibid.* 345), to Geoffrey of Lèves and Bernard, 1138 (PL 182:531), to Bernard, 1141 (PL 180:333), to the prior and the novices of Mont-Dieu (PL 184:305 and Dom J. M. Déchanet in *Scriptorium* VIII, 1954, p. 259). We know of three other letters through the replies of Bernard: Letters 85 and 86 (PL 182:206) and the preface to the *Apologia* (*ibid.* 895). A letter of Bernard to his friend is the cover-letter that accompanied *De Gratia et Libero Arbitrio* (PL 182:1001). Still another is the acknowledgement of receipt of the dossier on Abelard: *Letter* 327 (*ibid.* 533). We should have at least six letters of William addressed to Clairvaux, but there were many others: the *Vita Bernardi* lets us know that correspondence between Clairvaux and Rheims was frequent.

The limited dissemination of the anthologies and excerpts is self-explanatory in a period when this type of work was tending to give way to more systematic productions. Noteworthy, however, is the success of the commentary of the *Song of Songs* based on Ambrose, and of the treatise on the *Sacrament of the Altar*. Both, often as anonymous, were in circulation outside the Bernardine corpus. It must be admitted, however, that in their case from the very time of their composition, both were passed around by their recipients.

The treatise against Abelard is normally found in the dossier of the Council of Sens, among the works of Bernard.

Other works may be divided into two parts. His own commentary of the *Song of Songs* remained at the single-copy stage. The two tracts of faith, the *Mirror* and the *Enigma*, by reason of their theological character, are excluded from collections of spiritual writings, The *Meditations*, too, are still not widely known. On the other hand, the *Golden Epistle* and the two treatises on love have enjoyed great success. This they owe to the patronage of Bernard, a patronage from which the *Meditations* could hardly have benefited since their style and form differed too greatly from that of the Abbot of Clairvaux. Even though *On Contemplating God* is closely connected with the *Meditations*, it has still more the character of a treatise, especially when one compares it with *On the Nature and Dignity of Love*. This mere patronage of Bernard, however, does not suffice to explain the spread of these three works of William. There is the fundamental cause—the fact that they are works of profound spirituality.

Nevertheless the three treatises deserved a better fate. While the *Golden Epistle* was circulating on its own, the two others were progressively fused. Almost always *On Contemplating God* precedes *On the Nature and Dignity of Love*. The title given to the first is *On Love, On the Love of God* or something similar—for example, *On the Sweetness of Intimate Love* or *Soliloquy*. The second keeps its title for a longer time, but one also finds *On Charity, On the Art of Love*, or *Another Tract on Love*. This last is found in the Anchin manuscript which foreshadows the fusion, in the thirteenth century, of the two treatises into one. The copyists may indeed at times mark the beginning of the second by an ornamental initial letter which is rarely distinguishable from such letters indicating the paragraphs when the two treatises are placed together.

In the Bernardine corpus it was an easy matter to join *On Love* and *On Delight* and it was sometimes done. Here again it was the Anchin manuscript that opened the way.[27] As far as our knowledge goes, we must wait for the Horstius edition of Cologne in 1641 to present the three treatises explicitly as three parts of one and same work.[28]

Reading William is not easy. In order to grasp so original a thinker, it is necessary to adhere closely to the form of his expression. It demands sustained application, slow and reflective reading. One must put up with a vocabulary that is quite personal, with characteristic technical expressions and constructions that savor more of the oratorical style than of the written exposition, with a rattling of words and assonances and a use of methods that nonplus the modern mind. The rhetoric of the twelfth century is combined with one of the most original minds of the time. It may be added that the thinker, still in his beginning stages, is casting around for his ideas and their expression. Still more, this philosopher proceeds after the manner of an impressionist, by juxtaposing spots of color. A word, in his mind, necessarily brings with it all its connotations; which he might leave as simply an allusion or explains with a definition or a quotation. To penetrate William's thinking with all its nuances, or simply to arrive at an understanding of the man, it is necessary to subordinate oneself to this style and to make it one's own by patient labor. Reading aloud can be helpful, especially when one has caught the rhythm that singles out the essential words and stresses the abundance of the ideas.

To be faithful, the translation should pulse with these characteristics of style, temperament, and mind. It should also be as literal as

27. In it we find the treatise of St Bernard, *De Dilectione Dei*, followed by William's two treatises under the one title of *De Amore*.

28. *De Amore Dei* seu *De Diligendo Deo* libri tres. Liber primus *De Amore Dei* (alibi *De Contemplando Deo*): liber secundus *De Amore Dei* (alibi *De Natura et Dignitate Amoris*); liber tertius *De Amore Dei* seu *De Diligendo Deo*.

possible. Any error should lean toward excessive fidelity rather than extreme freedom, under pain of obscuring the physiognomy of the author, giving the thought a meaning not intended or one which will be only subsequently developed.[29]

The treatise, *On Contemplating God*, should not, therefore, be approached as if it were a book to be read without difficulty. The reader will discover it is best to submit to William's thought, remembering that his writings are food for reflection and meditation.

THE STRUCTURE AND CONTENT OF THE TREATISE

Writings of another age often present difficulties, and the present treatise is no exception. More than one copyist has found it disconcerting and it easily disturbs today's reader. For a better understanding of it, it is worthwhile to emphasize the principal modes of expression and the themes around which the work is constructed.

The division of the treatise

An attentive reading of *On Contemplating God* distinguishes two parts differing in subject and even in style. The first part, the more vehement, seems more personal and intimate, for it endeavors primarily to describe the desire that urged William on to the contemplation of God. The second part is more didactic; it reflects on the way in which God brings to realization the desire of his creatures. The style is noticeably modified; it is not always freer, but calmer and less abrupt.

Examination of the manuscript tradition confirms this impression and permits a precise determination of the place where the division

29. The translation takes the liberty of dividing the paragraphs which are veritable chapters.

must be made. At the same time, the division into paragraphs reveals the sections of the exposition.[30]

The analysis

The first part of the work might be entitled, "The Itinerary of the Soul Toward God"; the second, "The Holy Trinity, the Source of Love".

A short prologue which commences like a liturgical invitatory presents the object of the treatise: the contemplation of God in himself by detachment from all that binds one to earth. William describes his quest for God, his fruitless efforts to reach the divinity of the Word beyond the contemplation of the humanity of Christ and to attain to intimacy with God beyond the divine perfections reflected in creation. If, at times, he is given higher experiences, they are of but short duration and his soul falls back painfully on itself. William is thus led to question the nature of his love and the reason for these vicissitudes. He discovers the reason, under divine inspiration, in a distinction between the love of desire which, though meritorious, is anxious and painful, and the love of fruition which enjoys the presence of the beloved. This latter alone is the perfection of love.

Thus we find introduced a new section in this first part in which William treats of the perfection of love, providing a prelude to the more metaphysical considerations of the second part. This perfec-

30. The manuscript tradition is divided on this point into two homogeneous groups. In the first, to which the most ancient and in many respects, the most interesting, manuscripts belong, the text is divided into thirteen paragraphs the length of which varies from a few lines to several pages. This inequality attests to an initial desire to mark the manner in which the exposition was delivered, rather than to arrange a balance, in the text, of equivalent sizes. The second group divides the work into ten paragraphs. This division, which manifestly derives from the preceding, is the act of a logical mind that did not know how to penetrate the thinking of the author. In the manuscripts of the first group the cut between the two parts of the treatise can be recognized by an initial of a different color (v.g. Bruges 128).

tion is not a conclusion, a limit, but a perpetual ever deeper penetration into God. It consists in a perfect union of love between the Creator and the creature, involving a fundamental identity of wills. It is the *unitas spiritus*.

The first part concludes with a prayer in which William summarizes in bold outline his doctrine on the nature of love.

In the second part, William pursues his study of the perfection of love, but this time he views the question from the summits. To give an account of the union of love between God and man it is necessary to rise to the heart of the mystery of the Trinity, even to the consubstantiality of the divine Persons.

God first loved us and sent us his Son in order to move us, especially by his passion and death, to return the free gift of our love. To this external manifestation of divine love the secret motion of the Holy Spirit responds in the interior of our souls. It is he who, in giving himself to us, becomes our love, as he is the love of the Father and the Son in the bosom of the Trinity. It is by this union, by this *unitas spiritus* that, re-cast in the image of God, we know God with an experiential knowledge, in a connatural way that transcends all other knowledge. This long meditation ends with an ardent invocation to the Creator Spirit.

Before closing his treatise, William adds some details. Love should prove itself in works animated by faith, with God as both the principle and the term. A final description of the mystical experience leads William to insist again on its brevity, its elusive character, and its transcendence.

The treatise ends with a final outburst in praise of God as Principle, Wisdom and Beatitude, culminating in expressions of profound adoration.

All this can be summarized in the following schema:
I. The soul's itinerary to God: 1–8.
Prologue. The escape to God: 1.

A. The quest for God: 2–5.
    1. The desire for God: 2.
    2. The contemplation of the humanity of Christ: 3.

Such seems to be the plan of *On Contemplating God* when, amid the abundance of ideas and images, one pauses at the key words. Considerable pruning is necessary. In particular, one must leave aside all subordinate thoughts which have been grafted on to the main idea by a chance quotation, an assonance, an allusion, a reminiscence. One must also crystallize the body of the discourse and, in consequence, harden the expression of an extremely supple mind. Sometimes, even our interpretations go somewhat beyond the terms of the treatise and base themselves on other works which can throw light on the present text by showing in its maturity a thought which is here only in the first stage of development.

But after thus analyzing William's thinking, we must return to the text and savor all its density. The treatise is remarkably orchestrated. Let us know how to perceive the richness and diversity of its tones. Let us know, too, how to recognize beneath the basic melody, the return of the subordinate themes.

We shall then, in this short treatise, grasp all of William's doctrine. We shall understand why this book, devoted to the contemplation of God, speaks so much of love. To know presupposes a connaturalness of subject and object. Given the infinite distance between God and man, the latter cannot know God, truly and intimately, except by a gift of God—and this gift could be none other than God himself. It is by the indwelling of the Holy Trinity that we become one with him, entering, so to speak, into his knowledge and love. But just as the Holy Spirit constitutes the bond between the Father and the Son, so does he also play a major part in our union with God. And since he is love, it is by love that we are one with God and able "to see his face."

SOURCES

Holy Scripture

Like all the spiritual authors of the twelfth century, William of St Thierry thinks, lives, and speaks with the Bible.[31] It nevertheless remains difficult to determine precisely when the sacred text constitutes an immediate source, and when it simply gives texture to his language. These distinctions demand recognition.

In *On Contemplating God* we find explicit citations as fundamental or accessory arguments. An example is provided by his use of the

31. On the use of the Bible by monastic authors of the Middle Ages see Jean Leclercq, *The Love of Letters and the Desire of God* (New York: Fordham, 1961), pp. 87–109, and Father Dumontier, *Saint Bernard et la Bible* (Paris: Desclée, 1953).

text from John: "He first loved us." Far more numerous are the implicit quotations and among these we must make further distinctions. Some, varying in length, continue to enter the line of reasoning. Others seem like exclamations or effusions which arise spontaneously or during a pause in the exposition. Others again, are but a resurgence of the thought, or even of the word. Indeed, in the mind of William, words give rise to a whole scriptural context in which they find their complete signification or perhaps acquire only a certain shading. Finally, there is a great number of terms, expressions and pairs of words borrowed from Scripture. To what extent can we still speak of a scriptural source? When the Bible is the ordinary nourishment of the mind, it becomes the habitual source of thought and inspiration, often unconscious, of the writer's form of eloquence.

Also noteworthy is the fact that the quotations, whatever their form, do not always reproduce the sacred text exactly. Words are misplaced or changed, as if the memory had proved unfaithful. More often, the text is modified in order to continue and develop the discourse. William even paraphrases, and sometimes rather remotely, by taking only a word here and there from the passage that serves as his inspiration. At other times he follows Scripture closely, but quotes it in an equivalent manner.

Liturgy

As a liturgical office, the treatise begins with an invitatory—*Venite*. We do not have here a fortuitous simile, but rather an exact indication of one of the sources of the treatise. It is indeed fitting to juxtapose liturgical texts with Scripture; they are themselves in large part Scripture, but presented in a different light and with a particular meaning. If, in effect, the psalter furnishes the constant element of liturgical prayer, so too, the use of a psalm verse on a given feast gives it a special value, as does the frequent repetition of a verse throughout the course of the canonical hours. This relation of Scripture to the liturgical service should come under consideration in studying William's sources. However, it will not always be possible, either in his case or in that of his contemporaries, to determine whether the text became familiar from the singing of the Divine Office, or from choir, refectory, or cloister.

It should be remarked that the liturgical texts, as well as the scriptural texts properly so called, are utilized and not merely copied word for word. What is more, the quotations are usually corrected by a version of the Bible that is not that of the liturgical books.

The Latin Fathers

This also holds true in regard to his other sources of inspiration. William habitually fails to name them. Where he does indicate them, it is usually in veiled terms.[32] We have already met this in his treatment of Scripture. If we can easily guess that "the Apostle of your love" (10) might be John, it is more difficult to find Aratus in "the heathen poet" (11), Augustine in "one of those whom you enlightened" (12) and especially Scotus Eriugena in "one of your servants" (8).

This lack of precision or this absence of references, like the alterations of quoted or utilized texts, makes research on the sources a delicate task. We are often hesitant. The treatise is suggestive of endless rapprochements with the works of the Fathers, but in many cases it is merely a question of themes that are substantially common to all patristic thinking. Such, for example, is the case of the doctrine of the image of God in man, or of the conception of "nature" seen as "historic nature, including the passive, and not purely the obediential aptitude, for deification."[33] We will dwell, then, only on the more evident similarities, though without denying that William has been permeated with everything he read so carefully.

32. See the list, still provisory, of William's sources, in Dom J. M. Déchanet, *Guillaume de Saint-Thierry, l'Homme et Son Oeuvre,* Appendix II, pp. 200ff.; *id., Aux Sources de la Spiritualité de Saint-Thierry,* Bruges, 1940; *id.,* "Guillaume et Plotin" in RMAL, II (1946), pp. 241 and fol.

33. I. Hausherr, *Philautie* (Rome, 1952), p. 137.

C

A search for his sources reveals the breadth of his formation. Augustine is, perhaps, his preferred author. It is he who, in numerous passages, inspires William's style. He is the inspiration for the affective cast; he sets the tone of a colloquy with God. He is mentioned, although in a discreet way, and is most often quoted. William frequently draws on his thought, even when wandering somewhat far afield from his model.

It is worth noting that, from the thinking of Augustine, William retains primarily those elements which are consonant with the Oriental tradition, even those which had been already developed by Scotus Eriugena. Nevertheless, although he disregards the theory of the psychological analogies of the Trinity in man, his trinitarian doctrine is one point clearly of Augustinian and Occidental inspiration—the role of love in uniting the Father and the Son attributed to the Holy Spirit.

We recognize as contributions of Augustine the notion of love envisioned in man as a tendency of the image toward its Principle, the distinction between "love" and "the love of love" and the doctrine of the progress of love from desire to fruition. With regard to the virtues of pagans, the dependence is evident. Throughout the treatise, similarities in words, expressions and ideas reveal the extent to which the Abbot of St Thierry is familiar with the work of the Bishop of Hippo, particularly his *Confessions*, the *Treatise of the Trinity*, the *City of God* and *Letter 147*.

Along with Augustine, mention must be made of Gregory the Great. The relationship is certain between William and the "Doctor of the Desire for God". The doctrine that desire continues even in the state of blessedness is common to various authors upon whom the Abbot of St Thierry has drawn.[34] It is, however, in the very terms of Gregory that he has formulated it (6). Additional characteristics of Gregory are to be found in the succession of outbursts and

34. Gregory of Nyssa (see J. Daniélou, *Platonisme et Théologie Mystique* (Paris, 1954), pp. 294); Maximus the Confessor (see H. von Balthasar, *Liturgie Cosmique*, p. 273); Scotus Eriugena (*De Div. Nat.*, PL 122:615 A, 919 C–D, 1010 C–D); see also H. von Balthasar, *Parole et Mystère Chez Origene* (Paris, 1957), pp. 22–24.

relapses together with the tone in which William expresses them. Finally, has not the theme of knowledge through love, which is basic to the treatise, been drawn from the same source?[35]

Other authors could be mentioned, especially those who, in the wake of Augustine's *Letter to Paulinus*, *Letter 147*, have spoken of the vision of God—primarily Raban Maur. But William knows that the Greek Fathers had already treated the subject.

John Scotus Eriugena and the Greek Fathers

The literature of the Christian Orient had always attracted the Abbot of St Thierry. While he was drafting *On Contemplating God*, he must certainly have had access to numerous elements of Greek thought in the works of Scotus Eriugena. It is more difficult to specify the extent to which he was already in direct contact with the works of Gregory of Nyssa or Maximus the Confessor.

The influence of Eriugena is affirmed on almost every page of the treatise. In a large measure, it has contributed to the formation of William's style, singular in its sentence structure and vocabulary. There is a considerable number of apparently ordinary words and expressions which are frequently encountered in Scotus Eriugena. When compared with others that are characteristic, they betray their origin. Furthermore, in his style, William is much closer to the personal expositions of Eriugena than to the translations he made from the Greek. Nor have we overlooked the fact that he may have had at his disposal works of Eriugena which today are lost.

The system of Eriugena is built upon the Neo-platonic theme of emanation and return. Everything comes from God, subsists in him and flows back to him, *ex ipso, et per ipsum, et in ipso, et ad ipsum sunt omnia*. The echo of this leitmotiv of Scotus[36] is discernible in numerous passages of *On Contemplating God*. Nevertheless,

---

35. See St Gregory the Great, *Hom. XXVII in Evang.*, 4; PL 76:1207 A: *Dum enim auditia supercaelestia amamus, amata, jam novimus, quia amor ipse notitia es*

36. PL 122:679 A; 688 A; 1012 D; etc.

William restricts its application to the individual story of the soul; he does not take up the essential theme of *On the Division of Nature*. Eriugena here deals with the division and the original separation of natures and their reunion, "without confusion or admixture." This reunion is effected when creatures, deified by "theophanies," return to their Principle. God thus becomes "all in all." Even the characteristic term "theophanies" does not appear in William until later. Of this "immense metaphysical epic," William has fastened above all else upon this: "in the work of deification, charity constitutes the force par excellence which unites us to God and makes us like him."[37] In addition, he borrows from *On the Division of Nature* a definition of love which he prefaces by a discreet reference.

From Eriugena and other Eastern masters comes, too, for example, the distinction between *esse* and *bene esse*, the doctrine according to which "it is God himself who loves himself in us," and a few other themes.

Besides Scripture, liturgy, and the Latin and Greek Fathers should we not include some of the ancient writers among William's sources? William quotes once from Horace and, like Paul, from the poet Aratus. In spite of his pessimism in their regard, he does concern himself with the doctrine of pagan philosophers (12), thus attesting to his humanist formation. However, nothing borrowed from these doctrines is apparent in the text of *On Contemplating God*.

The Originality of William

In both form and substance, the treatise on contemplation is grounded on a wealth of information that denotes a cultivated, curious and eclectic mind. It was important to ferret out the sources of the work in so far as they can be recognized beneath a very homogeneous text that is sparing in explicit quotations—poor even in quotations properly so-called, except those from Scripture.

---

37. J. Pegon, in *Maxime le Confesseur, "Centuries sur la charité," Sources Chrétiennes*, 9 (Paris, 1953), Introduction, p. 53.

Undoubtedly, William will move forward in the construction of his philosophical system and especially in the elaboration of his spirituality, principally with regard to the Greek sources. However, in his very first work, two tributary streams can be recognized—the one Latin and predominantly Augustinian, the other Oriental.

It is this which, with his temperament and mental attitude, constitutes his originality in a century so rich and diverse. In regard to the past, he is to be found in a line which, after Gregory, numbers authors such as Bede and Ambrose Autpert. In this same line he can be compared to the Cluniacs, Odo and Odilo, both of whom lived the mystery of Pentecost, but with an ecclesiological note that is not found in William's works. On the other hand, he does not seem comparable to Romuald and Peter Damien, or to John of Fécamp or Anselm. Even in this current he stands out as being somewhat of the ascetic, but more especially on the mystical side. He utilizes freely his Dionysian sources, seeking less to describe the divine transcendence than to attain it. When he speaks about God he avoids Dionysius' vocabulary of superlatives. This deep-seated originality allows him to give to an eminently catholic doctrine the particular physiognomy which distinguishes him from his contemporaries—Peter the Venerable and Bernard, for example, or his immediate successors such as Hugh of Victor.

On Contemplating God IN WILLIAM'S WORKS AND IN THE HISTORY OF SPIRITUALITY

On Contemplating God remains a difficult book, even after prolonged study. In vain does one search out the structure of the treatise, sift the basic ideas, re-discover the essential sources; there always remains some obstacle to be cleared. It is as if we were dealing with a work that is incompletely formulated. William still needs to make his terminology more precise, sound out his ideas more thoroughly, and give them an expression more clear and systematic. This will be the work of a lifetime. *On Contemplating God* is like a prelude in which the major themes are lightly touched only fore-shadowing their final development. It would be an easy matter to pick out passages, or simply allusions, each of which announces some treatise yet to come. We have already noted the importance given to Trinitarian theology and to the question of grace, the necessity for faith, and the place of love in the spiritual life.

To localize On Contemplating God in the history of spirituality is too vast an undertaking. We shall simply outline its trend in one particular direction. One of the theological quarrels in which Hincmar played a leading role concerned the vision of God.[38] It provoked various opuscules and letters from Godescalc, Loup de Ferrières, Raban Maur, and, perhaps, Scotus Eriugena. Originally, the point at issue was to determine whether or not we shall see God with our material body or with a spiritual body. It was a return to a problem already proposed by Augustine.[39] But the discussions passed beyond the matter under dispute to border upon related subjects—such as ascertaining how each one will see God in himself and in his creatures, or preparing for the beatific vision by purity of heart, or distinguishing between the manifestations of God and vision of God as he is. These subjects are not foreign to On Contemplating God; the writings dealing with them must have been familiar to William. If it is somewhat difficult to reconcile, either in substance or form, the De Contemplando with the letter of Loup de Ferrières,[40] it must be realized that William could have taken only an idea of the latter regarding knowledge (God will be seen in himself and in each of his creatures) and used it in a concept of love.

In comparing his treatise On Seeing God with the On Contemplating God, we recognize the new aspect William gives to his work. The distinction in the titles already suggests it. Certain ideas

38. Cf. Dom M. Cappuyns, "Note Sur le Problème de la Vision Béatifique au IXᵉ Siècle" in RTAM I (1929), pp. 98–107.

39. St Augustine, Ep. XCII ad Italicam; Ep. CXLVII ad Paulinam; Ep. CXLVIII ad Fortunatianum; and also in De Civ. Dei, XXII.

40. Ep. XXX of the Duemeler edition; LXXX of the L. Levillain edition (Loup de Ferrières, Correspondance, II, p. 42; the collection Les Classiques de l'Histoire de France au Moyen Age, 16; Paris, 1935).

are similar, but the subject is no longer the same. A great many scriptural quotations are common to both, but they appear in developments that are noticeably different. All this, however, is secondary to the main point: seeking the possession of God which, in love and through love, far surpasses the natural capacity of man. Raban Maur, very learned and still more devout, seems quite dull beside William of St Thierry, a thinker, who follows the problem back to its principles and proposes a solidly constructed solution. We realize the distance that can exist between a choice culling of Scripture and the Fathers, intelligent though it may be, and a reasoned and well-informed theological construction. Around 1064, the subject discussed in the ninth century is reopened by Jean de Fécamp,[41] but on a more spiritual note that makes him akin to William. However, because of its brevity, his essay remains far removed from the constructive effort of *On Contemplating God*.

Even this effort has a source, in the sense that it reverts to a similar attempt during the time when the question of the *On Seeing God* was discussed. William develops Scotus Eriugena. His importance in the formation of William's ideas and often of their expression, authorizes us to speak of the "Eriugenism" of William. However, this word must not obscure the originality of the thinker, his power of assimilation, his freedom and, above all, the new cast of his philosophy, drawn from ancient sources. Apropos the identification of grace with the Holy Spirit, A. M. Landgraf has noted William's place, particularly in *On Contemplating God*, between Scotus Eriugena or Paschasius Radbertus on the one hand and Peter Lombard on the other.[42]

William, therefore, stands out for his intellectual effort, yet he does not cease to reveal himself as affective, almost sentimental. Better than many of his predecessors, he knew how to assimilate the very tone of his master, Augustine, whether quoting or imitating him. It is under this aspect that, in the literature of the soliloquies, we must place this work which has sometimes rightly been given the

41. Jean de Fécamp, to the Empress Agnes, PL 147:456.
42. A. M. Landgraf, *Dogmengeschichte der Frühscholastik*, I, 1 (Regensburg, 1952), p. 220.

title *Soliloquy of Bernard*.[43] In this field, William shows himself far more capable than other authors of the ninth to the twelfth centuries, doubtless because he is less a man of letters and more sincere. He even distinguishes himself from a man whose mind was rather close to his in certain respects—St Anselm. Several passages from the *Monologion* and especially from the *Proslogion* could have provided the occasion for an encounter between these two authors. But there is nothing of the kind, either in subject matter or form. The beginning of the *Proslogion* can be taken as characteristic. Despite many common terms, similar ideas—even in spite of the title *Excitatio Mentis ad Contemplandum Deum*—it remains something completely different. The logician cuts short his reasonings on the ascent to God; the metaphysician infuses love into all his developments.

Under this double aspect, that of the thinker and the man of heart, another parallel can be established with works of the second half of the twelfth century or later. The Abbot of St Thierry knows how to bring together both aspects, even though writers are soon to divide into two distinct camps. William's works reveal a degree of affection unattainable by the kind of pious writings which give free rein to sensibility while lacking doctrinal content. In his reasoning he preserves a liberty which will transcend preestablished logical schemes. The evolution begins to make its appearance only a few years after *On Contemplating God* with *On the Love of God* of Bernard who is, however, still close to his friend, but more methodical and more rational.

These qualities, which are rather of a personal order, betray themselves in a very original exposition. William re-opens the subject of *On Seeing God* by the combination of two themes. On the one hand, he considers the pure of heart who merit to see God as he is because they have become one spirit with him. On the other hand, he takes up the theme of God, the exemplary cause, abasing himself by "condescension" to all that is most intimately man's, so

43. The title *Soliloquia* is but one of the titles of the *De Contemplando* or of the *De Contemplando* followed by the *De Natura et Dignitate Amoris*. But this title is also given to the little text *In Lacu* (v.g. Brussels 1377).

that man may return to that which is most intimately God's. He realizes this in a two-fold way. First, man's unsatisfied desire to know leads into love which, when satisfied, assures at one and the same time both possession and vision. Then, the study of love in itself, on a more philosophical plane, leads to the concrete case of love in the bosom of the Trinity and in the manifestations of the Trinity to the intelligent creature. God, who is love, accomplishes the very object of *On Contemplating God*. Beginning from the Father, in the successive mediation of the Son and of the Spirit, and also in the concomitant mediation of the Son in the Spirit he accomplishes this by unity of nature and love, which makes a unity of knowledge possible. Of the two elements of knowledge the natural resemblance of an ontological order and the acquired resemblance of a moral order—the treatise develops the latter only in an imperfect manner. It perhaps does not show with sufficient clarity how love can be called knowledge. Then, too, when it places the emphasis on the unity that love establishes between man and God, it proceeds to steer the solution of the problem of contemplation towards an insertion of the loving activity of the soul into the circuit of the divine operations. It is perhaps here that in relation to the history of spirituality and the life of William, we find the most original element of *On Contemplating God*. Its place in the history of spirituality can be expressed concretely by situating it in a listing of treatises: *De Videndo Deo, De Contemplando, De Diligendo, De Caritate*. It is more difficult to find the formula that situates this first work properly in William's life. In the light of the preceding explanations perhaps we may choose this quotation, *ut sint unum*.

Jacques Hourlier OSB

THE BEGINNING OF THE TRACT OF
DOM WILLIAM, ABBOT OF SAINT THIERRY,
ON CONTEMPLATING GOD

"COME, LET US GO up to the mountain of the Lord, and to the house of the God of Jacob, and he will teach us his ways."[1]

Yearnings, strivings, longings, thoughts and affections, and all that is within me, come and let us go up to the mountain or place where the Lord both sees and is seen![2] But worries and anxieties, concerns and toils, and all the sufferings involved in my enslaved condition, all of you must stay here with the ass—I mean my body—while I and the lad—my intellectual faculties—hasten up the mountain; so that, when we have worshipped, we may come back to you.[3]

For we shall come back, and that unfortunately, all too soon. Love of the truth does indeed lead us far from you; but for the brethren's sake,[4] the truth of the love forbids us to abandon or reject

---

1. Is 2:3.   2. Cf. Gen 22:14.   3. Cf. Gen 22:5.

4. This consciousness that his responsibilities as abbot towards his community impeded his freedom in divine contemplation runs throughout the writings of William of St Thierry: e.g. *Meditation Eleven*, below pp. 161ff. *The Nature and Dignity of Divine Love*, chapter 8, trans. J. Cummings, *The Works of William of St Thierry*, Vol. 5 (Cistercian Fathers Series 15); *Exposition on the Song of Songs*, n. 51, trans. C. Hart, vol. 2, *The Works of William of St Thierry* (Cistercian Fathers Series 6), pp. 40f. This was an experience which William shared with his close friend, Bernard of Clairvaux. See *Exposition on the Song of Songs*, Song One, Stanza Three, note 10, *loc. cit.*, p. 41.

you. But, though your need thus calls us back, that sweet experience must not be wholly foregone on your account.

Desire for God

2. "Lord God of hosts, restore us; show us your face, and we shall be saved."[5] But alas, O Lord, alas! To want to see God when one is unclean in heart is surely quite outrageous, rash and presumptuous, and altogether out of order and against the rule of the word of truth and of your wisdom! Yet you are he who is supremely good, goodness itself, the life of the hearts of men and the light of their inward eyes. For your goodness' sake, then, have mercy on me, Lord; for the beholding of your goodness is of itself my cleansing, my confidence, my holiness. You have your own way, my Lord God, of saying to my soul: "I am your salvation."[6] Wherefore, Rabboni,[7] Master supreme, you who alone can teach me how to see the things that I desire to see, say to your blind beggar: "What shall I do for you?"[8]

And you know, since it happens only by your gift, you know how from the inmost depths of my being and after I have put away from me all striving after worldly honors and delights and pleasures, and everything else that can—and often does—arouse in me the lust of the flesh, or of the eyes, or that stirs up in me a wrong ambition[9]—you know how my heart then says to you: "My face has sought you: your face then will I seek. Do not turn your face from me; do not turn away in anger from your servant."[10] So look, O my helper of old and my unwearying defender! I know I am behaving outrageously, but it is the love of your love that makes me do so, as you indeed can see for yourself, though I cannot see you. And just as you have given me desire for yourself, if there is anything in me that pleases you, that also comes from you. And

5. Ps 79:20. For citations from the psalter we will follow the Vulgate Bible since this was the one with which William was familiar.

6. Ps 34:3.   7. Jn 20:16.   8. Mk 10:51.

9. 1 Jn 2:16.   10. Ps 26:8f.

even as your blind man runs towards you, you forgive him, and reach out your hand to help him if he stumbles over any obstacle.

The Humanity of Christ

3. Very well then! Let your voice testify deep down within my soul and spirit, shaking my whole being like a raging storm, while my inward eyes are dazzled by the brightness of your truth, which keeps on telling me: "No man shall see you and live."[11] For I indeed am as yet wholly in my sins,[12] I have not learned yet how to die to myself in order to live to you.[13] And yet it is by your command and by your gift that I stand upon the rock of faith in you, the rock of the Christian faith, and in the place where truly you are present. On that rock I take my stand meanwhile, with such patience as I can command, and I embrace and kiss your right hand that covers and protects me. And sometimes, when I gaze with longing, I do see the "back" of him who sees me; I see your Son Christ "passing by" in the abasement of his incarnation.[14]

But when in my eagerness I would approach him and, like the woman with the issue, am ready to steal the healing for my poor ailing soul by furtively touching even the hem of his garment,[15] or when like Thomas, that man of desires,[16] I want to see and touch the whole of him and—what is more—to approach the most holy wound in his side,[17] the portal of the ark that is there made,[18] and that not only to put my finger or my whole hand into it, but wholly enter into Jesus' very heart,[19] into the holy of holies, the ark of the covenant, the golden urn,[20] the soul of our humanity that holds within itself the manna of the Godhead—*then*, alas! I am told:

---

11. Ex 33:20.   12. Jn 9:34.   13. 2 Cor 5:15.
14. Ex 33:21ff.   15. Mt 9:20ff.   16. Cf. Dn 9:23.
17. Jn 20:24ff.   18. Gen 6:16.

19. For William to enter into the heart of Christ is to enter into the contemplation of the divinity of the Word, as is evident from the context here, and even more clearly from *Meditation Eight:* "The manna of your Godhead which you, O Jesus, keep within the golden vessel of your all-wise human soul, is your sweet heart!"—See below, p. 141.   20. Heb 9:3f.

"Touch me not!"[21] and I hear that word from the Book of Revelation: "Dogs outside!"[22]

Thus, and deservedly, my conscience harries and chastises me, forcing me to pay the penalty for my presumption and my wickedness. Then I return to my rock, the rock that is a refuge for the hedge-hogs[23] that bristle all over with sins. And once again I embrace and kiss your right hand that covers and protects me.[24]

Thus far I have perceived and seen, faintly enough indeed; and yet that slight experience has sufficed to kindle my longing afresh, so that I can scarcely now contain myself for hoping that one day you will remove your covering hand and pour out your illuminating grace,[25] so that at last, dead to myself and alive to you, according to the answer of your truth with unveiled face I shall begin to see your face,[26] and by that seeing shall be united[27] to you. O face,

---

21. Jn 20:17.   22. Rev 22:15.   23. Ps 103:18.

24. Compare this paragraph with n. 10 in William's treatise *On the Nature and Dignity of Love* (Cistercian Fathers Series 15).

25. "Illuminating grace" is an expression found quite frequently in William's works, especially in his *Exposition on the Song of Songs* (Cistercian Fathers Series 6), nn. 22, 47, 63, 71, 74, 80, 90, 101, 115, 141, 153, 158, 174, 201. In the preface to his commentary (n. 22) he distinguishes it from creative grace. The soul has been created in the image of God, triune (having memory, intelligence, and will) and one (one single substance). The soul has an aptitude to know and to love God. It is here that it is the image of God by creative grace. By the supernatural illumination of grace the soul can progressively come to know and love God. It is then the image of God by illuminating grace. This grace which is a sort of experiential knowledge of God pertains especially to the contemplative life. For William it is a very special gift, but one for which we can prepare ourselves. See note 55, p. 17, in *Exposition on the Song of Songs* (Cistercian Fathers Series 6).

26. *Revelata facie ipsam tuam faciem incipiam videre.* The nature of this very lofty state of contemplation is developed more fully by Guerric of Igny (who frequently uses the expression *revelata facie*—Sermons 13: 7; 19:6; 46:4) in his *Third Sermon for the Feast of the Epiphany*; *The Liturgical Sermons of Guerric of Igny* I (Cistercian Fathers Series 8), pp. 83ff. It belongs to wisdom as the consummation of a life of faith and virtue. See the Introduction to Guerric's Sermons where this is developed by John Morson and Hilary Costello: *loc. cit.*, pp. ivff.

27. *Affici*: this is a difficult word to render. It expresses the twofold idea of a very intimate union and a blow or wounding. God by his illuminating grace

face, happy face that merits thus to be united to yourself through seeing you! It builds in its heart a tabernacle for the God of Jacob and does everything according to the pattern shown it in the mount![28] Here with truth and fittingly it sings: "My heart has said to you, 'My face has sought you; your face, Lord, will I seek.' "[29]

So, as I said: by a gift of your grace looking at all the nooks and limits of my conscience, I desire only and exclusively to see you, so that all the ends of my earth may see the salvation of their God;[30] and that, when I have seen him, I may love him whom to love is to live indeed. For, faint with longing, I say to myself: "Who loves what he does not see?[31] How can anything be lovable which is not in some way visible?"

The divine perfections in creation

4. But he who longs for you, O Lord adorable and lovable, is at once confronted with the qualities that make you lovable; for from heaven and earth alike and by means of all your creatures these present themselves to me and urge me to attend to them. And the more clearly and truly these things declare you and affirm that you are worthy to be loved, the more ardently desirable do they make you appear to me.

But alas! This experience is not one to be enjoyed with unmitigated pleasure and delight; rather, it is one of yearnings, strivings, and frustration, though not a torment without some sweetness. For just as the offerings I make to you do not suffice to please you perfectly unless I offer you myself along with them, so the contemplation of your manifold perfections, though it does give us a measure of refreshment, does not satisfy us unless we have yourself

---

"affects" the soul. At the same time the soul is stricken, wounded, "affected"— and united, "glued" to God. Sometimes William will say *affici tibi*, as here and in the opening lines of his *Exposition on the Song of Songs* (Cistercian Fathers Series 6), p. 4: "drawn to you," placing the accent on the union; and sometimes *afficitur a te*, "affected by you," placing the accent on God's action.

28. Cf. Ex 25:40. 29. Ps 26:8. 30. Is 52:10. 31. 1 Jn 4:20.

along with it. Into this contemplation my soul puts all its energies; in the course of it I push my spirit around like a rasping broom.[32] And, using those qualities of yours that make you lovable like hands and feet on which to lift my weight, with all my powers I reach up to you, to you who are Love supreme and sovereign Good. But the more I reach up, the more relentlessly am I thrust back, and down into myself, below myself.

So I look at myself, and size myself up, and pass judgment on myself. And there I am, facing myself, a very troublesome and trying business.

And yet, O Lord, when all is said and done, I am quite positive that, by your grace, I do have in me the desire to desire you and the love of loving you with all my heart and soul.[33] Thus far you have brought me—to the point, that is, of desiring to desire you and of loving to love you. But when I love like that, I don't know what I love. What does it mean, to love love and to desire desire? If we love anything, it is by love that we love; and it is by desire that we desire all that we desire. But maybe when I love love, it is not the love that I love—the love, that is, with which I love that which I want to love and by which I love everything that I do love at all— but it is I myself whom I love in the act of loving when in the Lord

---

32. *Scobo vel scopo spiritum meum. Scopo* could equal the classical latin, *scabo*, which would mean to grate or rub or strike together as one might strike together a couple of stones to bring forth a spark or it could equal *scopo (scopare)* with the idea, as it is taken in the translation here, of cleaning up, sweeping out. The former interpretation might have more support from a parallel usage in William's *Golden Epistle: Scabendo spiritum nostrum donec encalescat*, which could easily relate the action with the production of a flame. Here William might be inspired by a text from Cassian in his *First Conference* (n. 19, ed. A. Pichery, Sources Chrétiennes, 42, p. 101) and both of them taking their inspiration from Psalm 76:7.

33. Mt 22:37. In this sentence we seem to have the rather clumsy efforts of a young writer to develop a play on words in the imitation of some master (was William here perhaps trying to imitate the eloquent style of Bernard? Certainly Bernard often employed assonance, but usually with much more grace and charm) : *Tandem tamen Domina certa certus sum per gratia tuam desiderium desiderii tui et armorem et amoris tui habere me.* . . . William senior in the *Exposition on the Song of Songs* would arrive at a much more mature use of this device of literature.

I praise and love my soul,[34] this soul which beyond all doubt I
should loathe and detest if I found it anywhere else but in the Lord
and his love.

But what, then, of desire? If I say: "I desire to be desirous," then
I find myself desirous already. But is it that I desire the desire for you
as if I had never previously had it? Or do I desire a desire greater
than that which I already have?

Vicissitudes of contemplation

5. So, when my inward eyes grow blurred like this, and become
dim and blind, I pray you with all speed to open them, not as
Adam's fleshly eyes were opened, to the beholding of his shame,[35]
but that I, Lord, may so see your glory[36] that, forgetting all about
my poverty and littleness, my whole self may stand erect and run
into your love's embrace, seeing him whom I have loved and loving
him whom I have yet to see. In this way, dying to myself, I shall
begin to live in you. O may this blessedness of being in you be given
to me, for whom the worst thing possible is to be in myself!

But, Lord, make haste, don't loiter![37] For the grace of your
wisdom—or the wisdom of your grace—has its short-cuts. For
there, where there are no rational arguments or lines of thought to
lead one on and upwards step by step, up to the torrent of your
delights[38] and the full joy of your love—there, I say, he to whom
you grant it, he who seeks faithfully and persists in knocking,[39] there
of a sudden he may often find himself arrived already! But, Lord,
when something of this joy falls to my lot—and it is all too seldom

---

34. Cf. Ps 33:3.   35. Gen 3:7.   36. Ps 62:3; Ex 33:18.

37. William here quotes the eleventh responsory which is sung at vigils on
the second Sunday of Advent. For William like the other Fathers of the
Cistercian school the liturgy was a great source of inspiration; there is evidence
that even the inspiration that came to them from the Scriptures was mediated
to them through the liturgical celebrations. Compare the present text with
Psalm 39:18.

38. Ps 35:9.   39. Mt 7:7f.; Lk 11:9.

that it happens—but when it does, Lord, then I cry aloud and shout: "Lord, it is good for us to be here! Let us make here three tents, one for faith and one for hope and one for love!" Do I ever know what I am saying when I say: "It is good for us to be here!"? But then forthwith I fall to the ground as one dead, and when I look around me I see nothing.[40] I find myself just where I was before, back in my sorrow of heart and affliction of soul.[41] Till when, O Lord, till when? How long must I seek counsel in my soul and be vexed in my heart every day?[42] How long will your Spirit thus come and go in mortal men, never remaining with them, blowing where he will?[43] But when the Lord leads back the captives of Sion, then shall we be as men comforted, then will our mouth be filled with joy and our tongue with gladness![44]

Meanwhile, I have been a foreigner too long. I have dwelt with the inhabitants of Kedar,[45] very much an exile have I been in soul. Yet deep within my heart the truth of your consolation and the consolation of your truth reply: "There are two loves, the love of desire and the love of delight. Desiring love is sometimes rewarded with sight; the reward of sight is delight, and delight earns the perfecting of love."[46]

I thank you, then, who by your grace have deigned to speak to your servant's heart[47] and give at least a partial answer to my anxious questions. I receive and embrace this token[48] of your

---

40. Cf. Mt 17:4 and parallels; see also Rev. 1:17.

41. Sir 1:14.   42. Ps 12:1f.

43. Jn 3:8 collated with Gen 6:3. William here is speaking of the Holy Spirit. The graces of contemplation are given by God when he wills and how he wills. In this sense the Holy Spirit does not rest in a stable manner with man. William longs for the heavenly future where the joy of the Lord will be perfect and perduring.

44. Ps 125:1f.   45. Ps 119:5f.

46. Here William intimates that divine illumination has given him an answer to the question that he is troubled with in the opening paragraphs of this treatise, namely, in the distinction between the love of desire and the love of fruition, the one preparing for the other and leading toward the perfection of love.   47. Cf. Ruth 2:13.

48. *Arram.* Cf. *Exposition on the Song of Songs*, no. 20, *op. cit.* p. 15. Also, 2 Cor 1:22.

D

Spirit, and with it joyfully look forward to the fulfillment of your promise, of which it is the guarantee. So I desire to love you, and I love to desire you; and in this way I press forward, hoping to make him my own who has made me his own.[49] That is to say, I hope one day to love you perfectly, you who first loved us,[50] you the love-worthy, you the lovable.

The endless perfecting of love and desire

6. But does this perfecting of love for you, this consummation of beatitude in loving you, ever or anywhere exist, O Lord? Is the soul that thirsts for God as for the fount of life [51] ever so satisfied and so fulfilled that it can say: "It is enough!"?[52] No matter who or where the man may be who says: "It is enough," I feel pretty certain that there is some lack in him! But what perfection can there be where any lack of that sufficiency obtains?[53] Is perfection never and nowhere to be realized? But then what about the unrighteous, Lord? Will they possess your kingdom?[54] Now an unrighteous man is one who has no desire, no awareness of his debt, no understanding of your love for us proportionate to the love for you which it is possible for a rational creature to possess. Again, it is certain, surely, that the blessed seraphim, for whom their nearness to your presence and the clearness of their sight of you has earned the name of "burning ones"[55]—and that indeed they are—it is

---

49. Phil 3:12.   50. 1 Jn 4:10.

51. William seems here to be quoting Psalm 41:3. However it is well to note in the Vulgate text we find *Deum fortem vivum* rather than the more logical *fontem* which William has used here.

52. Prov 30:15f.

53. See William's treatise on the *Nature and Dignity of Love*, no. 11 (Cistercian Fathers Series 15) for a concrete example of the young monk who, satisfied with the first touches of God, says: "It is enough" and rests there. William says tersely of this situation: "Where one ceases to go forward, he begins to fall back." *Ubi desit proficere incipit deficere.*

54. 1 Cor 6:9.

55. See Denis the Areopagite, *De caelesti hierarchia*, 15; trans. Scotus Eriugena: *Seraphim caeligus ardentes ex cognominatione significare.*—PL 122:1065.

certain, I say, that they love you more than he who is lesser in the kingdom of heaven. Here in the kingdom of heaven is someone who is I will not say the least in it, but someone, anyhow; and he desires to love you as much as ever you can and should be loved by anyone; and this maybe is that into which the angels desire to look.[56] So this happy "lesser one," whoever he is, desires to love you as much as all those others do who love you more than he does. And this he does, not in a spirit of rivalry but by way of devout and godly imitation. Moreover, if he makes progress in love, the more his inward eyes are enlightened[57] and the more he grows to be at home with the interior realities, so much the more, provided he is not ungrateful and unrighteous, does he perceive and understand with increasing sweetness that you can be loved more, and that he himself, debtor as he is, can love you more, and that even he can love you as much as do the cherubim and seraphim.

But he who desires what he cannot get is in a pitiable state; and misery like that is far removed from the kingdom of bliss. So, up there, everyone who desires anything attains it. What shall we say to that?[58] What, I repeat, shall we say? Speak, I beg you, Lord, for

56. 1 Pet 1:12. For a patristic commentary on this "desire of the angels" see St Gregory the Great, *Moralia in Job*, 28, 91.

57. Eph 1:18.

58. Rom 8:31. William poses here with great acuity the problem of the insatiable desire inherent in love. One wishes to know God to the full extent of his loveableness or at least as much as he can be loved by a creature. Love is never satisfied. It wishes to grow, be as great as the love of others who love more. On the other hand how could one reconcile perfection, the happiness of heaven with a lack of fulfillment or satisfaction? The perfection of love demands that it be satisfied. Whence the different questions and now the oppositions present themselves. One cannot in the face of infinite good ever consider himself completely satisfied; he ought always to desire more. But on the other hand perfection demands fulfillment, the quieting of all desires. Is it necessary then to say that the perfection of love will never be attained? In heaven all do not love with the same ardor. Can one in seeing others, for example the burning Seraphim, who love more than he does not desire to love as much as they? William goes on to give his answer to this. For him desire does remain in love but it is a desire which is quieted, satisfied, in that the one who loves less loves the love of him who loves more and by that very fact makes that greater love his own.

your servant listens![59] Those who are in the kingdom of God, both great and small, each one in his own order, do they not love, and do they not desire to love? And does not the unity of love permit that there shall also be diversity?[60] While he, to whom it has been given so to do, loves more ardently, does not his "lesser" brother love, without any envy, the good he desires for himself wherever he beholds it? And is it not certain that in this way he has in its entirety, however great that is, the love which he loves in him who loves?[61]

For the truth is: it is Love who is loved. He, out of the abundance and the nature of his goodness, fills with the same grace those who love and love together, those who rejoice and rejoice together, but he does not give to all in the same measure. And the more plentifully he pours himself into the faculties of those who love him, the more able does he make them to receive himself. He satisfies, but never surfeits them; and the satisfaction itself does not lessen their desire, but rather increases it, although it takes away from it the worry and distress. For, as I said, Love is he who is loved. It is he who, by the flood of his delights,[62] relieves the man who loves him from all his distress, whether it be that of surfeit which comes of satisfaction, or of the anxiety that desire breeds, or of the envy that grows out of zeal. As the Apostle says, he enlightens them "from glory to glory,"[63] so that in the Light they see light,[64] and they understand love in Love.

For here is the fount of life that flows without cease and never runs dry. Here is the glory, here are the riches in the house of your blessed Lover,[65] for here he who desires finds what he wants forthwith, and he who loves finds what he loves. He, moreover, who

---

59. 1 Sam 3:10.

60. Bernard of Clairvaux in his *Apologia to Abbot William* answers this question, as does William himself here, in the affirmative, developing the reasons for this. See *Cistercians and Cluniacs: St Bernard's Apologia to Abbot William*, nn. 6ff.; trans. M. Casey in *The Works of Bernard of Clairvaux*, vol. 1 (Cistercian Fathers Series 1), 40ff.

61. Bernard of Clairvaux also shared this conviction that love truly possessed what it loved. See *Apologia*, n. 8; *op. cit.*, p. 43.

62. Ps 35:9.

63. 2 Cor 3:18.

64. Ps 35:10.

65. Ps 111:3.

desires loves always to desire, and he who loves desires to love always. And for him who desires and loves, O Lord, you make what he desires so to abound that the desirer is vexed by no anxiety, nor does he who has plenty ever have too much. And, O Lord, I ask you: is not this the eternal way of which the Psalmist sings: "See if there be a way of wickedness in me, and lead me in the way eternal"?[66] This relationship, this is perfection. To travel always thus is to arrive. So your Apostle first said: "It is not that I have already attained, or am already perfect, but I press on, hoping to take hold of that for which Christ has taken hold of me. One thing alone I do: forgetting what lies behind and straining forward to what lies ahead, I press on towards the goal, to the prize which is God's call to life supernal in Christ Jesus."[67] He said that first, I say. And after that he added: "Let all of us who are mature be of this mind."[68]

Unity of spirit

7. And this loving of yours, O kind Creator, with which you love those who love you, comes from the sweetness of the loving-kindness that you have towards your creature. And it inspires in your lovers both the desire to love you, and the love with which they love both to desire and to love you. For, when you love us, you are in no wise affected either for or by us; but you simply are what you are. You are the same One who you always are, for whom to be is to be good, but good for yourself and in yourself, and in yourself also for all your creatures. We, on the other hand, when we love you—we, for whom in some wretched way it is possible to exist and yet not to love you, to be, that is to say, and to be evil— we, I say, when we love you are affected by you, toward you and in you.[69] But for you, who are always the same,[70] nothing is added if

66. Ps 138:24.   67. Phil 3:12ff.   68. Phil 3:15.

69. When the soul is "affected . . . in you"—*in te afficimur*—drawn into God, united to God, the union creates an affect in man—"affected by you"—*a te afficimur*—and part of this affect is that the soul strives towards God, seeks God, "affected toward you"—*ad te afficimur*. See above n. 27, pp. 39f.

70. Ps 101:28.

by loving we advance toward you, nothing is taken away if we fall away from you. Nevertheless when you love us, it is only for yourself, for the inalienable rule of ultimate justice allows even us to love nothing outside you.

And surely, when a great grace is given to someone who loves God, it is possible for his love to reach the point of loving neither you nor himself for himself, but you and himself for yourself alone.[71] And by that he is re-fashioned in your image, after which you created him.[72] For by the truth of your unique nature, and by the very nature of your truth, you can love yourself only for yourself; you can love neither angel nor man otherwise than for yourself.

O the incalculable blessedness of the soul that merits so to be acted on by God, that through unity of spirit she loves in God, not just some property of his, but God himself, and even loves herself only in God! Like God, she loves and approves in herself what God must approve and love, that is to say, himself. Or, to put it in another way, she loves and approves in herself that which must be loved by both God the Creator and by his creature. In a word, neither the name of love nor love itself belongs by right to anyone, nor is owed to any, save to yourself alone. O you who are true Love, love-worthy Lord, this also is the will of your Son in us, this is his prayer for us to you his Father: "I will that, as you and I are one, so may they themselves be one in us."[73] This is the goal, this is the consummation, this is perfection, this is peace, this is "the joy of the Lord,"[74] this is joy in the Holy Spirit,[75] this is the "silence in heaven."[76]

71. Cf. with St Bernard's degrees of love. The third is to love God only for himself; the fourth, which is the summit, is to love one's self only for God. *On the Love of God*, nn. 26, 28; *The Works of Bernard of Clairvaux*, vol. 7 (Cistercian Fathers Series 19).

72. Gen 1:26.

73. Jn 17:21f. William habitually applies this text to the unity of the human spirit with God without any explicit reference to the unity of Christians among themselves. See below, n. 11, p. 55; *Meditation Eight*, p. 142. Cf. Cassian, *Conferences*, 10, 7.

74. Mt 25:21; Jn 15:11.   75. Rom 14:17.   76. Rev. 8:1.

In fact, as long as we are in this life, it is given us to enjoy the ineffable peace of the "silence in heaven"—that is, in the soul of the righteous which is the seat of Wisdom[77]—only on occasion, for the space of half an hour, or "for scarcely half an hour."[78] But with the thoughts that remain the soul's attention remains fixed on you, as in the observance of a perpetual feast day.[79] In that blessed and eternal life, however, of which it is said, "Enter into the joy of your Lord,"[80] there alone will the enjoyment be perfect and perpetual. And the bliss then will be proportionately greater, in that by that time all the things that now seem to hinder or retard it will have been done away; and the eternity of her love will be secure for ever, her perfection will be inviolable, and her bliss such as cannot be corrupted.

Prayer: the nature of love

8. Come to us, Love, and take possession of us! Drive from before your face[81] all those foul infections which the lust of the flesh and of the eyes, and the pride of life,[82] have brought to birth in our affection like a rank overgrowth of bastard shoots—in this affection, I repeat, which is called love in us, but which too often is corrupted in the soul created by and for you. For you alone it is created and implanted in us; and, when it resists the natural law and cries out

---

77. William here is taking an adaptation of Prov 12:23 (Septuagint) from Gregory the Great: *Anima justi sedes sapientiae*—Homily 38, *On the Gospels*, 2; PL 76:1282. We find also in Gregory's *Homilies on Ezechiel*, 2, 14, another passage which could be inspiring William here: *Coelum quippe est anima justi . . . ; quo ergo quies contemplativae vita agitur in mente, silentium fit in coelo. . . , sed quasi media hora* —PL 76:957.

78. Rev 8:1.

79. William here is quoting a difficult text from the Vulgate Psalter, Ps 75:11. He applies the same text in his *Exposition on the Song of Songs*, n. 43, where he brings out more clearly that "the thoughts that remain," the remembrances, are the past consolations which remain in the memory: "the joy of dwelling on the remembrance of consolation once possessed "—*The Works of William of St Thierry*, vol. 2 (Cistercian Fathers Series 6), pp. 33f.

80. Mt 25:21.   81. Ps 67:3.   82. 1 Jn 2:16.

against it, it earns for itself such names as gluttony, lust, avarice, and the like.[83] But as long as it continues incorrupt and obedient to the law of its being, it is directed on to you, to whom only love is due.

In fact, as one of your servants has said, the love of the rational soul is "a movement, a quiet abiding, or an end, in which the will neither seeks anything beyond that which it has, nor reckons anything to be desirable."[84] But he who seeks for anything beyond you or above, as though it were a better thing than you, is seeking for something that does not exist, for there is nothing better nor lovelier than you. That is why such a person makes himself a nonentity when he flees from you, whose is the sole authentic claim on love, and indulges in fornication and those other alien passions with —as I said before—their alien names. For love, as has been said, and as I must repeat, is directed on to you alone, and it is in you alone that anyone who truly is exists at all. There in you, in you alone, is the quiet safe abiding, for "to fear God" with the chaste fear of love, "and to keep his commandments, this is the whole man."[85]

A cry to God

9. So, then, may all unrighteousness take its departure from my soul, that I may love the Lord my God with all my heart, and with all my soul, and with all my strength![86] Let all jealousy[87] depart from me, lest I should love anything along with you that I do not love for your sake, true Lord and truly only Love! For, when I love anything for your sake, I love not it, but you for whose sake I love that which I love. For you truly only are the Lord.[88] To be ruled by

---

83. See Gal 5:19ff.

84. Cf. Scotus Eriugena, *De divisione naturae,* I, 74; PL 122:1519.

85. Eccles 12:13.

86. Deut 6:5; Lk 10:27.

87. William uses here an unusual word: *zelotopia.* It is found in Num 5:29. St Benedict uses it in RB (64:16) in the adjectival form.

88. Ps 85:10.

you is for us salvation. For us to serve you is nothing else but to be saved by you!

The love of God and the sending of the Son

10. Now how is it we are saved by you, O Lord, from whom salvation comes and whose blessing is upon your people,[89] if it is not in receiving from you the gift of loving you and being loved by you? That, Lord, is why you willed that the Son of your right hand,[90] the Man whom you made strong for your own self, should be called Jesus, that is to say, Savior, for he will save his people from their sins.[91] There is no other in whom is salvation[92] except him who taught us to love himself when he first loved us,[93] even to death on the cross.[94] By loving us and holding us so dear he stirred us up to love himself, who first had loved us to the end.[95] This is the righteousness of the sons of men: "Love me, for I love you." One seldom meets a person who can say: "I love you, *in order that* you may love

89. Ps 3:9.

90. Ps 79:18.

91. Mt 1:21. In this n. 10 William begins to speak at length of Christ, the Savior, the Second Person of the Blessed Trinity, showing how he and all that he has done provokes love and thus how man can attain to a deep intimacy with God through the contemplation of God. In the following number he will consider the role of the Third Person of the Blessed Trinity, the Holy Spirit in the work of salvation, of which the Father is the beginning and the end. We find a similar development in one of St Bernard's letters to Thomas, the Provost of Beverley: "As a pledge of his love you have the Spirit and you have the faithful witness to it in Jesus, Jesus crucified. A double and irrefutable argument of God's love for us. Christ died and so deserves our love. The Holy Spirit works upon us and makes us love him (*Spiritus afficit et facit amare*). Christ has given us a reason for loving himself, the Spirit power to love him."—Letter 107, n. 8; PL 182:246f.; trans. B. S. James, *The Letters of St Bernard of Clairvaux* (London: Burns and Oates, 1953), Letter 109, p. 162. The whole of this beautiful letter might well be read with these sections of William's treatise.

92. Acts 4:12.   93. 1 Jn 4:10.

94. Phil 2:8.   95. Jn 13:1.

me!"[96] But, as the servant of your love proclaims and preaches, you who first loved us did this, precisely this. You first loved us so that we might love you. And that was not because you needed to be loved by us, but because we could not be what you created us to be, except by loving you. Having then in many ways and on various occasions spoken to the fathers by the prophets, now in these last days you have spoken to us in the Son, [97] your Word, by whom the heavens were established, and all the power of them by the breath of his mouth.[98] For you to speak thus in your Son was an open declaration, a "setting in the sun"[99] as it were, of how much and in what sort of way you loved us, in that you spared not your own Son, but delivered him up for us all.[100] Yes, and he himself loved us and gave himself for us.[101]

This, Lord, is your word to us, this is your all-powerful message: he who, while all things kept silence (that is, were in the depths of error), came from the royal throne,[102] the stern opponent of error and the gentle apostle of love. And everything he did and everything he said on earth, even the insults, the spitting, the buffeting, the cross and the grave, all that was nothing but yourself speaking in the Son, appealing to us by your love, and stirring up our love for you.

96. William sees in this formula: "I love you in order that you may love me!" the expression of a love that is supremely disinterested: "I love you in order that responding to my love you can find your happiness." Such was the love of Christ for us as William tells us here in the following lines and again more explicitly in his *Treatise on the Sacrament of the Altar*: "All that our Redeemer accomplished during his mortal life had for its end to evoke our love; not that he had any personal need of it. He did it only for our good. But having received the mission to make us blessed he cannot do it unless we love him."—c. 5; PL 180:251.

97. Heb 1:1f.   98. Ps 32:6.

99. Ps 18:6. St Bernard makes the same application of this text to the incarnation: *On the Song of Songs*, 6:3 (Cistercian Fathers Series 4); *First Sermon for the Feast of the Epiphany*, 1 (Cistercian Fathers Series 10).

100. Rom 8:32.

101. Gal 2:20.

102. Wis 18:14ff. These lines are sung at the opening of the mass on the Sunday within the octave of Christmas.

Love is not constrained

For you, O God, our souls' Creator, knew that this affection
cannot be forced in the souls of the sons of men, but has to be evoked.
And this is for the obvious reason that there is no freedom where
there is compulsion, and, where freedom is lacking, so too is
righteousness. But you, O righteous Lord, you who wish to save us,
you never save or condemn anyone otherwise than justly. You are
the author of both our judgment and our cause. Sitting upon your
throne and judging righteous judgment, you judge the righteousness
that you yourself have made.[103] Thus will every mouth be shut, and
the whole world be made subject to God,[104] when you have pity on
him on whom you will have pity, and extend mercy to him to
whom you will be merciful.[105] We could not with justice have been
saved, had we not loved you, nor could we have loved you, save by
your gift. You willed, therefore, that we should love you. So, Lord,
as the Apostle of your love tells us, and as we ourselves have said
before, you "first loved us";[106] and you love all your lovers first.

The love of God in the sending of the Holy Spirit

11. Now we on our part hold you dear by the affection of love[107]
which you have implanted in us. But how is it with you? Do you,
the Creator of all things, both of the good dispositions and of the
souls that are to be affected by them, do you love those whom you
do love by some extraneous, incidental activity? And are you, the

---

103. Ps 9:5.   104. Rom 3:19.

105. Ex 33:19, which is cited by St Paul in Rom 9:15.

106. 1 Jn 4:10.

107. Here again William uses the word, *affectus*. When we love God—most
especially in the case of the mystical *affectus*—we are "affected" by him; our
soul undergoes a change by the very fact that it loves. It is informed by God
and receives the impression of God on it. But God is not "affected" by what
he loves, when he loves a creature.

Maker of all men and all things, in some way, in some respect, affected in so doing? It is unthinkable! It would be ridiculous and contrary to faith to impute such a thing to the Creator of all! Well, then, how do you love us, if you do not love us with love? But, O you who are the One supremely good and the ultimate Goodness, your love is your goodness, the Holy Spirit proceeding from the Father and the Son! From the beginning of creation he has been borne upon the waters[108]—on the tossing souls of men, that is—offering himself to all, drawing all to himself.[109] And by breathing into and upon them, by warding off things harmful and supplying things useful, he unites God to us and us to God.[110] Your Holy Spirit, who is called the Love, and the Unity, and the Will of the Father and the Son, dwells in us by his grace[111] and implants in us the charity of God;[112] and through that charity he reconciles God to us. And thus he unites us to God through the good will that he breathes into us. And with us this vehement good will goes by the name of love, by which we love what we ought to love, namely you. For love is nothing other than a vehement, well-ordered will.

The Spirit of Adoption

So, then, love-worthy Lord, you love yourself in yourself when the Holy Spirit, who is the Love of the Father for the Son and of the Son for the Father, proceeds from the Father[113] and the Son. And that love is so great that it is unity, and the unity is such that it is oneness of substance[114]—that is the Father and the Son are of the

---

108. Gen 1:2.   109. Jn 12:32.

110. It is this action of the Holy Spirit which at one and the same time is the love of God for us and creates and enkindles our love for God. In his "affecting" us, in his touching us—by his inspirations and by his aspirations, God enables us to love him. See William's *Tract Against Abelard:* "When the spirit of man is 'affected' by the Holy Spirit, he becomes one spirit with him, and by that same action he is loved and he loves."—PL 180:261.

111. Rom 8:11.   112. Rom 5:8.   113. Jn 15:26.

114. William here uses a technical transliterated Greek word: *omousion.*

same being. And you also love yourself in us by sending the Spirit of your Son into our hearts, crying: "Abba, Father!"[115] through the sweetness of love and the vehemence of good intention that you have inspired. This is how you make us love you, or rather, this is how you love yourself in us. We first hoped, because we knew your name, O Lord;[116] we gloried in you as Lord and loved the name of the Lord in you.[117] But now, through the grace inbreathed into us by the Spirit of your adoption,[118] we have confidence that all that the Father has is ours also. So, through the grace of adoption, we invoke you now under the same name as your only Son invokes you by right of nature. But because all this derives exclusively from you, O sovereign Father of lights,[119] for whom to love is to do good and from whom comes every good endowment and every perfect gift, you, I say, love yourself in us, and us in yourself, when we love you through you. We are made one with you just insofar as we are worthy to love you and—as we said just now—become sharers in the fulfillment of your Son's prayer: "I will that, as you and I are One, so these also may be one in us."[120] For we are your people, Lord, God's People, as your Apostle says,[121] making the heathen poet's words the vehicle of good, so that only the savor of the good thought should be sensed. We are, I say, God's offspring,[122] we, all of us, are gods and sons of the Most High[123] through a kind of spiritual kinship. We claim for ourselves a closer relationship with you, because through the Spirit of adoption[124] your Son does not scorn to be known by the same name as we, and because with and by him, taught by saving precepts and schooled by God's ordinance, we are bold to say: "Our Father, who art in heaven."[125]

You, therefore, love us insofar as you make us lovers of yourself, and we love you insofar as we receive your Spirit, who is your Love,

---

115. Gal 4:6; Rom 8:15.   116. Ps 9:11.   117. Ps 5:12.

118. Rom 8:15.   119. Jas 1:17.   120. Jn 17:21.

121. Acts 17:28f.   122. Aratus, *Phaen.*, 5.   123. Ps 81:6.

124. Rom 8:15.

125. Mt 6:9. William uses here the same introductory words which are used by the priest at the celebration of the Eucharistic liturgy: *"Praeceptis salutaris moniti et divina institutione formati, audemus dicere."*

and let him lay hold of and possess all our secret affections, transmuting them into the perfect purity of your truth, and the truth of your purity, into full concord with your love. And this union, this adherence, this enjoyment of your sweetness will be such that our Lord, your Son, will call it unity, in saying: "That they may be one in us."[126] And so great is the dignity of this unity, and so great its glory, that he goes on to say: ". . . as you and I are one."[127] O the joy, the glory, the riches, the pride of it! For even wisdom has its own sort of pride when it says: "Riches and honor are with me, proud strength and righteousness."[128]

Love and blessedness

But what is there more incongruous than to be united to God by love, and yet not to be so in blessedness? For only those who love you truly are truly and uniquely and singularly happy, and they are perfectly happy, who love you truly and perfectly. On the other hand, no one is happy in any sort of way who does not love you. "Blessed are the people who possess such things," they said; but they lied, for he alone is blessed who owns God as his Lord.[129] For what in fact is happiness? Does it not consist in wanting only what is good, and having all one wants? Then to want you, to want you vehemently—that is, to love you and to love you exclusively, for you will not tolerate being loved along with any other thing whatever, carnal or spiritual, earthly or heavenly, that is not loved for your sake—to want you thus is to want nothing but what is good; and that is tantamount to having all one wants. For everyone possesses you just insofar as he loves you.

126. Jn 17:21.

127. Jn 17:11.

128. Prov 8:18.

129. Ps 143:15. In the Vulgate text one finds an opposition between the first part of the verse—it speaks of the temporal happiness of those whose outlook is wholly earthly—and the second part—the elect whose joy and glory is to have Yahweh for their God.

Love and knowledge

United, then, to God by love and blessedness alike, we understand that salvation is of the Lord indeed, and that your blessing is
upon your People.[130] Therefore, O ever-present Father, we offer
you our prayers, our sacrifices and our vows, and everything that
we possess through Jesus Christ your Son; for we believe and know
that all the good in us derives from you, through and for you,
through him from whom we have our very being.[131] All these
things we believe and understand, as far as they can be understood,
through the operation of your Holy Spirit dwelling in us.[132] He, as
we have said, breathes in us when, and as, and in such measure as he
wills,[133] and thus conforms and unites our spirit to himself. We are
his work, created for good works;[134] and he becomes our sanctifier,
our justification, and our love. For he himself is the love by which
we reach out to you, and by which we embrace you. And yet, O
Majesty transcending understanding, to the soul that loves you, you
do seem understandable. For though no faculty of soul or spirit
can ever comprehend you, nevertheless, the man who loves you
in his loving understands you totally, in all your greatness—if
indeed totality can be where there are no parts, or quantity where
there is no sort of measure, or understandability where these things
are not.[135] But, when we love you, your Holy Spirit truly acts upon

130. Ps 3:9.

131. A clear acknowledgment of the universal mediation of our Lord
Jesus Christ. In this William uses phrases similar to those customarily used in
the conclusion of the prayers or collects offered at the Eucharistic liturgy and
the office.

132. Phil 1:19; Rom 8:11.

133. Jn 3:8.

134. Eph 2:10.

135. When William in his writings speaks of our enjoying here on earth a
union with God which is very exalted and which seems to equal that of heaven
he almost always adds a corrective to what in his expressions could have been
too audacious by showing the difference that exists between the experience of
God in this life and the beatific vision. See for example, below, *Meditation
Three*, n. 6, p. 105; *Meditation Six*, n. 5, p. 127.

our spirit; through his indwelling we possess the love of God shed
abroad in our hearts.[136]

And when your love, that is, the love of the Father for the Son
and the love of the Son for the Father—the Holy Spirit, when he
dwells in us, he is to you that which he is—love. And he turns
toward himself and hallows all the "captives of Sion,"[137] that is to
say, all the affections of the soul. And, when he does all that, we
love you, or you love yourself in us, we affectively and you effectively,[138] making us one in you, through your own unity, through
your Holy Spirit whom you have given us. So it comes to this: that
as for the Father to know the Son is nothing else but to be what the
Son is, and for the Son to know the Father is simply to be what the
Father is (whence comes the Gospel saying: "No one knows the
Father save the Son, and no one knows the Son except the
Father"[139]), and as for the Holy Spirit to know and understand the
Father and the Son is simply to be what the Father and the Son are,
so is it with us. We were created in your image.[140] Through Adam
we have grown old in unlikeness; but now through Christ we are
being renewed in that image day by day.[141] So for us who love God,
I tell you, to love and fear God is nothing other than to be of one
spirit with him.[142] For to fear God and keep his commandments,
that is the whole of man.

Prayer asking for the Holy Spirit

O you who are adorable, tremendous, blessed, give him to us!
Send forth your Spirit, and we shall be made, and you will renew
the face of the earth![143] For it is not in a flood of many waters, in the
disturbance and confusion of our moods, which are as many in

136. Rom 5:5.   137. Ps 125:1.

138. "We affectively and you effectively"—this is one and the same act
considered under its two aspects, passive and active. Actively, God acts and
effects the soul evoking its love. Passively the soul is affected, wounded, united
to God by an illumined love of him.

139. Mt 11:27.   140. Gen 1:26.   141. 2 Cor 4:16.

142. 1 Cor 6:17.   143. Ps 103:30.

number as they are different in kind, that we shall draw near to God.[144] Lord, that disaster, the punishment of Adam's seed, has gone on long enough! Bring in your Spirit on the earth, let the sea draw back, let the wilderness of ancient condemnation draw back, and let the parched earth appear,[145] thirsting for the fount of life![146] Let the dove come, the Holy Spirit, when the great black bird has been driven out, and is hunching over his kill! Let the dove, I say, come with the olive branch, proclaiming peace with the branch that speaks of renewal and light![147] May your holiness and hallowing make us holy, may your unity unite us and, through what is indeed a sort of blood relationship, may we be united to God who is love[148] through the name of love. We shall be made one with him through the power of this name.

The true philosophy

12. But it is important, Lord, that we should know how one loves you. For, in point of fact, as one of those whom you enlightened says, many people "love the truth when it shines upon them but, when it rebukes them, then they do not love it."[149] And many people cultivate righteous feelings, but do not behave at all in the same way. They approve the truth, and love it in itself; but they do not put it into practice in themselves. Do they then truly love you, O God, true Righteousness? Do these love you in truth?

The philosophers of this world sought earnestly in ancient times for truth, affectively through love, effectively through action, so that it could be rightly said of them: "The love of virtue made good men hate to sin."[150] But the fount and wellspring of true righteous-

---

144. Ps 31:6.   145. Gen 1:9.   146. Rev. 21:6.

147. Gen 8:6ff.   148. 1 Jn 4:8.

149. St Augustine: *Amant eam lucentem oderunt eam redarguentem—Confessions*, 9, 23, 34.

150. Horace, *Letters*, bk. 1, Letter 16, 52; trans. E. Wickman, *Horace for English Readers* (London: Oxford University Press, 1930), p. 300. William cites this same text from Horace in his *Exposition on the Song of Songs*, n. 105 (Cistercian Fathers Series 6), p. 84.

E

ness is from you. It returns to you as to its end, and without you all human righteousness is only as soiled linen.[151] So those who did not love you are convicted of not loving righteousness; for, though they had love of a sort and had some honest actions to their credit, they nevertheless lacked the faith that works by love.[152] And, because their love (such as it was) and their good actions neither sprang from the fountain of true righteousness nor led to its end, these men went ever more hopelessly astray as they ran ever faster off the track. For the Way, O Father, is your Christ, who said: "I am the Way, and the Truth, and the Life."[153]

Your Truth, then, who is also the Way to and by whom we go, your Truth thus expresses the true divine philosophy in its truest, simplest form: "As the Father has loved me, even so have I loved you. Abide in my love. If you have kept my commandments, you will abide in my love, even as I also have kept the commandments of my Father and remain in his love."[154] Here is "the Beloved of the Beloved," of whom we read in the psalm,[155] here where the Father loves the Son[156] and the Son abides in the love of the Father, fulfilling his commandments to the uttermost. Again "the Beloved of the Beloved," when the beloved disciple loves Christ, his Master, fulfilling his commandments to the uttermost and remaining steadfast in this will even when it involves his death. Enlightened by his truth and love, he turns everything to good account, making good use of all things, good, bad, or indifferent, as Christian virtue should. For, as has been said before us, virtue is "the good use of free will,"[157] and "virtue's task is to make good use of the things that we could also use for ill."[158]

It is, therefore, in order that there may be no defect in charity that we are told to love our neighbor, according to the law of perfect love. Just as God loves only himself in us, and we have

---

151. Is 64:6.   152. Gal 5:6.   153. Jn 14:6.

154. Jn 15:9f.   155. Ps 67:13.   156. Jn 3:35; 5:20.

157. St Augustine: *Bonus usus liberae voluntatis, quae virtus est.—Retractiones*, I, 9, 6.

158. St Augustine: *Opus virtutis est bonus usus istorum quibus etiam non beneuti possumus.—De libero arbitrio*, 2, 19, 50.

learned to love in ourselves only God, so we are to begin now to
love our neighbor "as" ourselves.[159] For in our neighbor we love
God alone, even as we love him in ourselves.

The Spirit blows whither he will

But why, Lord, all these words? My wretched soul is naked and
cold and benumbed, it longs to warm itself at the fire of your
love. I have no garment to put on; to cover my nakedness I am
constrained to gather these poor rags from anywhere I can, and
sew them together.[160] And unlike the wise woman of Sarepta who
collected a couple of sticks, I out of my wide wilderness and the
great emptiness of heart have collected only these few tiny twigs; so
that, when I do come to the tabernacle of my house,[161] I may have a
handful of flour and a vessel of oil to eat before I die.[162]

Or maybe, Lord, I shall not die as quickly as all that! It may be
rather that I shall not die at all, but live, and declare the works of
the Lord.[163] So I stand in the house of solitude like the lone wild ass,
having my dwelling in the salty land.[164] I draw in the breath of my
love, I open my mouth in your direction, I breathe in the Spirit.[165]
And sometimes, Lord, when I, as if with eyes closed, gasp for you
like this, you do put something in my mouth, but you do not
permit me to know just what it is. A savor I perceive, so sweet, so
gracious, and so comforting that, if it were fulfilled in me, I should
seek nothing more. But when I receive this thing, neither by bodily
sight nor by spiritual sense nor by understanding of the mind do you
allow me to discern what it is. When I receive it, then I want to
keep it, and think about it, and assess its flavor; but forthwith it has
gone. Whatever it was, no doubt I swallowed it down in the hope

---

159. Mt 22:39.   160. Gen 3:7.
161. Ps 131:3.   162. 1 Kings 17:9ff.
163. Ps 117:17.
164. Accommodation of two texts: Jer 2:24 and Job 39:6.
165. Ps 118:131.

of eternal life. But I pondered long on its effect on me, and in so doing I wanted to transfuse into the veins and marrows of my soul a sort of vital sap: I wanted to be rid of the taste of every other affection, and savor that alone, for evermore. But it very quickly passed. And when, in seeking or receiving or experiencing this, I try to make my memory retain the more precise impressions of its features, or even, since my memory is fallible, to help it by writing something down, this attempt only forces me to recognize that here is what you say about the Spirit in the Gospel: "And you do not know whence he comes nor whither he goes."[166] For whatever the particular features of the experience may have been, I have wanted to commit them to memory, so that I could in a way go back to it, and take it to myself again whenever I was so minded, and so submit this power to my will whenever I chose. But every time this happens I hear the Lord say to me: "The Spirit blows whither he will."[167] And knowing even in myself that he breathes not when I will, but when he himself wills, I find everything devoid of taste and dead. And then I know that it is to you alone, O Fount of life, that I must lift up my eyes,[168] that I may see light only in your light.[169]

Towards you, then, Lord, are all things turned—and may my eyes be among them![170] May every step that my soul takes be towards you, in you, and through you. And when my strength, which is nothing, fails,[171] may my very weaknesses still pant for you! But in the meantime, Lord, how much longer are you going to put me off? How often must my wretched, harassed, gasping soul trail after you? Hide me, I beseech you, in the secret place of your face away from the troubles of men, protect me in your tabernacle from the strife of tongues![172]

But now the ass is braying again, and the lads are clamoring![173]

---

166. Jn 3:8.   167. *Ibid.*   168. Ps 122:1.

169. Ps 35:10.   170. Ps 140:8.   171. Ps 70:9.

172. Ps 30:21.

173. William here harkens back to the opening lines of this soliloquy or dialogue with God on contemplation as the needs of his own body and of his community call upon him to bring this to a close. See above, n. 1.

A closing prayer

13. Now, therefore, Lord, in complete faith I worship you. You who are God, the one Cause of all that is, the Wisdom whence the wiseness of every wise man comes, the Gift whence every happy man derives his happiness. It is you, the only God, whom I honor and bless and adore. It is you whom I love, or love to love, whom I long for, with all my heart, and all my soul, and all my strength.[174]

Every one of the angels and good spirits who loves you, loves me too—me, who also love myself in you; this I know. I also know that everyone, who abides in you[175] and can have knowledge of the prayers and thoughts of men, hears me in you, in whom I also return thanks for their glory. Everyone who has you for his treasure helps me in you, and it is not possible for him to envy me my share in you. Only the apostate spirit takes pleasure in our wretchedness, and counts our benefit his bane; for he has fallen away from the common good and from true happiness, and is no longer subject to the truth. Hating the common good, he therefore rejoices in isolation, hugging a joy belonging to himself alone.

You, therefore, God the Father,
　　by whom as Creator we live,
You, Wisdom of the Father,[176]
　　by whom we have been made anew and taught to live wisely,[177]
You, Holy Spirit, whom and in whom we love,[178] and
　　so live happily, and are to live yet more so,

---

174. Deut 6:5; Lk 10:27.

175. Jn 15:4.

176. 1 Cor 1:24.

177. The grace of God which pours down upon us from Christ refashions us into the likeness of God. The wisdom of which William speaks here is above all that which comes from mystical experience where the soul "touches" God and gains a certain "taste" for God and the things of God.

178. When the Holy Spirit enters into us and animates our love it is he who loves in us and it is then that we love in him.

You, who are Three in one Substance, the one God,
 from whom we are,
 by whom we are,
 in whom we are,
You, from whom we departed by sinning,
 to whom we were made unlike,
but away from whom we have not been allowed to perish,
You, the Beginning, to whom we are returning,
 the Pattern we are following,
the Grace by which we are reconciled,
You we worship and bless!
 To you be glory for ever!
 Amen.

HERE ENDS THE TRACT OF
DOM WILLIAM, ABBOT OF SAINT THIERRY,
ON CONTEMPLATING GOD

PRAYER

INTRODUCTION

FOLLOWING THE TWO TREATISES, *On Contemplating God* and *On the Nature and Dignity of Love*, the Reuil manuscript (Mazarine 776) contains a text of about a page and a half in length, entitled "The Prayer of Dom William." Everything in the disposition of the text testifies to the fact that this short piece of writing formed a part of the original manuscript. As one reads he sees how perfectly it is connected to William's two treatises. We would be surprised at not finding this in the other manuscripts if we did not already know what had happened to other works of William. Like the *Meditations*, the *Prayer* did not find its way into the Bernardine corpus either because the copy did not come from Clairvaux or because the subject and style made it difficult to attribute to Bernard.

The *Prayer* is not given in any list of William's works. This does not, however, allow us to deny his authorship. We have, by way of a guaranty, the Reuil manuscript, which is meticulous in its transcription, precise in its indications, and exact in its attributions. It situates this writing as a conclusion to a series of his works as a sort of signature. No one other than Dom William could be the author of the *Meditations*, the *Treatise on Contemplation* and the *Treatise on Love*.

A reading of the *Prayer* justifies the title. It can be asked if William is not starting another *On Contemplating God*, which was probably written at the same time; the style, the expressions and the words are found to be identical. The ideas, too, are common to both. He treats of seeking the face of God; he speaks again of the creation of man in the image of God. There is the same straining toward God in which progress alternates with regression. He stresses the role of the Word Incarnate and the Holy Spirit. And William makes similar borrowings from the works of the ancient philosophers.

Nevertheless, the *Prayer* is distinguishable from the two treatises that precede it; it is shorter though not just a résumé or a condensation. In spite of many resemblances, it is an original work. Not content with specifying certain ideas, that of knowledge-love, for example, it proceeds to tackle new subjects. William speaks of "the insight of reason or of love"; he encourages one to understand "not so much by the effort of reason as by the affection of love." He also speaks of true adoration and of the transcendence of God which surpasses all conception. He studies "the place of God" and, taking the words "my Father and I are one," he situates this "place of God" in the consubstantiality of the Holy Trinity. It is regrettable that he did not develop further this subject which is not given much attention by theologians of the twelfth and thirteenth centuries.

If, then, the *Prayer*, in many respects, comes close to the treatise, *On Contemplating God*, it also adds to it by greater exactness in terms and by additional ideas. This provides the only clue as to the date. It practically coincides with the writing of *On Contemplating God* and *On the Nature and Dignity of Love*, but a little later. The manuscript of Reuil shows the order by placing the *Prayer* in third place. We can thus date the *Prayer* around 1122.

The exact date, however, is of secondary importance, as this work marks no turning point in William's thinking. Its object is simply to ascertain where God can be found. Standing high on the mountain where God sees and is seen, William looks toward heaven in order to scrutinize the place where God dwells. There are no divisions that help one to distinguish the ideas that fit so closely together. We must analyze the text carefully if we are to recognize a structure, part of which is just barely indicated by the use of a more affective tone in the preamble and the conclusion that form the framework of the dissertation.

The preamble is an appeal for a full and single-minded love of God. The heart of the matter is subdivided into three parts. First, William strives to direct toward God an undivided attention. He employs the analogy of corporal vision to explain the knowledge of God. From this he concludes to the necessity of a specified object, near at hand. Then a brief scriptural quotation serves as a transition to the second part where he considers heaven where God lives. This is the heart of the *Prayer*. He quickly rises to the unity of the divine Persons, the consubstantiality of the Trinity and the divine transcendence. The few lines that follow place the Incarnation within this vision of God. The conclusion follows quite naturally, then suddenly changes to end on a dry, almost disagreeable tone that in reality conceals an invitation to aim at the summits.

St John's Gospel constitutes the principal source of the *Prayer*. We can also recognize several quotations from the Psalms, from Genesis, the Song of Songs and from the end of the Canon of the Mass. They are the same books and texts utilized in *On Contemplating God*. Only the Song constitutes a new contribution.

It would be of interest to know who gave William his inspiration for this little dissertation on God's place, but there is nothing to indicate it. Ordinarily, theologians explain why God, who is beyond time and space, cannot be contained in a place. They remain on the physical level, not rising with William to the very bosom of the Trinity. In his *Sixth Meditation*, William dwells more at length on the "place of God."[1]

The origin of another idea in the *Prayer* causes difficulty—that of divine truth.[2] An explicit though vague quotation sends us back to the philosophers of antiquity who defined truth. The text that most resembles it would be a definition of the true by the stoic Zeno, cited by Augustine, "We can perceive as true only a representation imprinted in the soul, arising from a real object, but such that would not exist if it did not result from a real object."[3] *The Prayer of*

---

1. See below, pp. 125ff.
2. See below, p. 73.
3. St Augustine, *Contra Acad.*, II, V, 11.

Dom William then would allow us to add a Greek philosopher to the sources of the Abbot of Thierry. Together with the notion of "the place of God" in consubstantiality, and the idea of a contemplation absolutely stripped of every sensible element, this unusual quotation gives special interest to this short text. On the other hand, the desire to love God, to see him—this need to arrive even at that which is most intimate in the Trinity through the Word Incarnate and the Holy Spirit—ties in completely with *On Contemplating God*.

Jacques Hourlier OSB

A PRAYER OF DOM WILLIAM

LORD JESUS CHRIST, the Truth and the Life,[1] you said that in the time to come the true worshipers of your Father would be those who worshiped you in spirit and in truth.[2] I beseech you, therefore, to free my soul from idolatry. Free her, lest in seeking you she should fall in with your companions,[3] and begin to stray after their flocks, during the sacrifice of her praise.[4]

1. Jn 14:6.

2. Jn 4:23. For William adoration in spirit and truth corresponds to "spiritual prayer" where the soul experiences God himself without the intermediary of any image or thought, where all "carnal" reality has been excluded, even the sacred humanity of Christ. See *Exposition on the Song of Songs*, n. 17; trans. C. Hart, *The Works of William of St Thierry*, vol. 2 (Cistercian Fathers, Series 6); *Golden Epistle*, nn. 173ff.; trans. T. Berkeley, *The Works of William of St Thierry*, vol. 4 (Cistercian Fathers Series 12). From this point of view images and corporeal representations during prayer constitute a certain degree of idolatry.

3. "Your companions"—this could be understood as the sacred humanity, the human acts of God in Christ, or the images we might form of these or of the divine Persons themselves. In the sense in which William here prays for pure prayer, giving one's self up to the consideration of these during prayer would be "to stray" and undesirable. Another reading, "her companions" (Pain de Cîteaux 23, p. 16) which can be justified from the mss. fits in also with William's thought. The companions in this case would be those of the soul, the imagination, the memory and concupiscence, as William says elsewhere (*Golden Epistle*, 62; *Exposition on the Song of Songs*, 17; *op. cit.*, p. 14). In this case the doctrine would be the same; for the soul to follow after the images coming from the imagination and the memory would be to adulterate the purity of the "sacrifice of praise."

4. *Sacrificium orationis*—a favorite expression of William which he uses frequently in his writings: *Meditation Ten*, 4, below p. 153; *Golden Epistle*, 64; *Commentary on the Epistle to the Romans* (PL 180:637).

No, let me rather lie down with you, and be fed by you in the noon-day heat of your love.[5]

By a certain natural sense derived from her First Cause the soul dreams—after a fashion—of your face, in the image of which she was herself created.[6] But because either she has lost the habit or never acquired it of not receiving another image in place of it, she is receptive when, in the time of her prayer, many other images offer themselves.

But when she strives to fix her attention on this face, not seeing it, sometimes she experiences that her effort has been anticipated by it. Often though it is only in the heavy sweat of her brow that she can eat her bread, laboring under the ancient curse.[7] And often, too, it is neither this way nor that with her but poor and starving she is compelled to return to the house of her poverty.[8] For either she attains her object quickly or, with equal speed, she fails. For it is with her as with the eye.[9] For the pupil to see, it is not enough for it to emit from itself a natural ray, or that the way of the air it traverses should be pure and clear. This ray must also fall as soon as possible upon the body at which it is aiming and on which it is to end. If it does go further, it loses vigor and, being no longer able to keep its object properly in focus, this single ray breaks up in many pieces and, being thus divided, perishes.

So is it with the intention in contemplation or in prayer. If the understanding of reason or of love has not received something definite from you that it can quickly put before itself where its affections can rest and its attention find an object, and where it can pour out the fruits of its devotion, then contemplation grows faint,

---

5. Song 1:6.   6. Gen 1:27.   7. Gen 3:17ff.

8. We have here neatly distinguished three possibilities which can occur in the prayer of a fervent soul. Sometimes it finds God almost immediately, God has so to speak anticipated its efforts. Often it must labor for a long time before the divine light comes as a recompense to its efforts. Again the case occurs that in spite of its effort the soul is frequently left at the end of prayer without having any real experience of God.

9. The ancients, including such writers as St Augustine, thought that perception by the sense of sight came about by the eye emitting a ray which attained its object and brought about the vision.

prayer waxes cold, attention falters, understanding becomes weak, and reason can do nothing.

But what have I in heaven? And, besides you, what do I desire upon earth?[10] For if in prayer I look for you in that heaven, beautiful indeed, and yet corporeal, which I see above me, I make the same mistake as if I sought you on the earth beneath my feet. If I seek you in any place, or as outside a place, either I include you in the place you made, or I exclude you from it. If I envisage for you my God, any form whatever, or anything that has a form, I make myself an idolater.

O Truth, answer, I implore you! "Master, where do you dwell?" "Come," he said, "and see."[11] "Do you not believe that I am in the Father, and the Father in me?"[12] Thanks be to you, O Lord! We have achieved something after all! We have found your "place"! For your "place" is your Father, and you are the Father's "place"! In this place you are localized. But this localization of yours, this limiting in space, is far more lofty and mysterious than any absence of place. This localization is the unity of the Father and the Son, the consubstantiality of the Trinity.

What then? Have we found "a place for the Lord"[13] in one way only? By no means. Do all you can, my soul, not so much by the exercise of reason as by the activity of love. And if the place of God is God, if this localizing of the Trinity is the consubstantiality, rid yourself of all the usual ideas about locality and place, and get firmly hold of this: you have found God in yourself. He himself shows that this is so—he who is all the more truly and surely, as he is of himself, in himself, through himself what he is. And, as the philosophers of old expressed it with reference to the truth: "He has being by such right that nothing exists that could possibly challenge his right to be." What is there more certain, more dependable, than this, by which our intention may orient itself and on which our affection may lay hold?

But again, if sometime in our prayer we clasp the feet of Jesus[14]

10. Ps 72:25.
11. Jn 1:38ff. William takes up this same question in *Med.* 6:6, below, p. 128.
12. Jn 10:38; 14:10.
13. Ps 131:5.
14. Mt 28:9.

and, attracted to the human form of him who is one Person with the Son of God, develop a sort of bodily devotion, we do not err.[15] Yet, in so doing, we do retard and hinder spiritual prayer. He himself tells us, "It is expedient for you that I go away. If I do not go away, the Paraclete will not come to you."[16]

If, however, we give way completely to laziness and sloth, and out of the depth of our ignorance cry to God, as out of a dungeon; and if we want to be heard even when we are not seeking the blessed face of him to whom we cry, and if we do not care whether he is angry or appeased when he gives us what we want, as long as we get it—well, a man who prays like that must be content with what God gives. He does not know how to ask God for a great thing, so it is nothing great that he receives.

And so it ends.

---

15. In more than one place William speaks of this prayer which he considers to be imperfect but which he recognizes to have a true value. See e.g., below, *Meditation Ten*, 4, pp. 152f ; *Exposition on the Song of Songs*, 17; *op. cit.*, p. 14; *Golden Epistle*, 43.

16. Jn 16:7.

MEDITATIONS

F

INTRODUCTION

WRITING TO THE CARTHUSIANS of Mont-Dieu,[1] William of St Thierry enumerates his works, among which he names the *Meditations: Meditationes Novitiis ad Orandum Formandis Spiritibus non Usquequaque Inutiles.* After mentioning two treatises, *On Contemplating God* and *On the Nature and Dignity of Love*, and then a little book, *Libellus, On the Sacrament of the Altar*, he goes on to indicate the *Meditations*, which, he says, are not absolutely useless for forming the minds of novices in prayer.

In the Reuil manuscript[2] we find the *Meditativae Orationes Domni Willelmi Abbatis Sancti Theodorici* which correspond perfectly to what William says of this work. The title, so precise, written in a very careful hand, constitutes an initial proof of authenticity, but one has only to read the text to be convinced that this is indeed from William's pen. Vocabulary, style, images, themes—all are his. After reading *On Contemplating God* the *Meditations* reveal a similar exposition, more loosely constructed, less developed in its doctrine,

1. *The Golden Epistle, The Works of William of St Thierry*, vol. 4 (Cistercian Fathers Series 12), Preface.

2. Paris, Bibl. Mazarine 776, fol. 1–23. The text is incomplete. It breaks off at the top of a page, after two and a half lines, in the middle of a sentence. The forgetfullness of the copyist? Or, perhaps, he had only an incomplete text to copy. All the rest of the page is blank although some fifteen lines would have sufficed to finish the text.

but abounding in parallels. The *Life* of William further confirms the authenticity and title of the *Meditations*.[3]

No other manuscript has transmitted this work to us. It must be concluded that the Carthusians who received it from their friend restricted its circulation to a very few cloisters. Certainly there was no reason here to fear theological quarrels, for in it William shows himself very reserved. Rather, they might have regarded it as rather personal revelations whose secret was to be reserved to those who would appreciate them.

Its dissemination begins with printing.[4] By including them in his *Library of the Cistercian Fathers*, Tissier[5] assured the preservation of the *Meditations* and their future passage into the *Latin Patrology* of Migne.[6] Tissier, furthermore, divided the text into twelve distinct meditations, to each of which he gave a title; or rather indicated its tenor with more or less success. These divisions and titles have been retained in the translation presented here.

It may be asked if such a presentation is legitimate. The manuscript offers no indication to justify it. It has no divisions other than paragraphs which habitually go to the line and are always designated by a fitting sign.[7] There is no numbering system which distinguishes subjects. The one employed here is taken from the edition of Robert

3. *Vita Willelmi* (Paris, National Library, lat. 11782, fol. 340–341): "He composed a lengthy treatise entitled, *Meditations*, in which he employed many different themes, rather than a single approach, to say many things of God while examining his own conscience in many ways."

4. On the dissemination, cf. André Adam, *Guillaume de Saint-Thierry, Sa Vie et Ses Oeuvres* (Bourg, 1923), p. 13, 15. André Wilmart, "La Série et la Date des Ouvrages de Guillaume de Saint-Thierry" in *Rev. Mabillon*, XIV (1924), p. 167 and note 3.

5. Edition of 1662, vol. IV, col. 22–41; edition of 1669, vol. IV, p. 1ff.

6. PL 180:205–248. There are two editions in accordance with the manuscript: *Meditativae Orationes*, text and translation by M. M. Davy, Paris, 1934 (Bibliothéque des textes philosophiques), and R. Thomas, Chambarand, 1964 (Pain de Cîteaux, 21 and 22).

7. This sign is between an F and the modern paragraph sign. It seems to be especially useful when the preceding paragraph finishes at the end of the line, and even more so when the scribe does not go all the way to the line.

Thomas.[8] There are no sub-titles, not even the rubric, *Alia*. The twelve paragraphs of the work do not constitute a series of meditations in the sense understood by a mind formed to the *devotio moderna*, nor in the sense understood by an editor accustomed to collections of systematic meditations. Quite the contrary, they form one whole, and only the last paragraph ends with a doxology: "he who has begun the good work shall also perfect it, he who lives and reigns through all the ages of ages."

These *Meditations* were therefore to be, as is stated in the *Life*, "a lengthy treatise," extremely free, in which the author "employs many different themes rather than a single approach." The editors were able to propose a subject for each of the meditations they sorted out. Their initiative, though sometimes fortunate, is not wholly satisfying, because each of the paragraphs develops several ideas. Conversely, throughout the entire writing, some themes recur, particularly that of the desire for the face of God which forms the very basis of the work.

Even though the *Meditations* are one entity, the treatise has absolutely nothing systematic about it. It must be realized that the author never intended to devote himself to an exposition which would develop an idea or lead a soul to contemplation. Does he not say that he simply wants to help those who are learning to pray? We are not yet in the age of methodical prayer. Here, as in other writings, William's meditation develops, or rather, unwinds in spirals around certain fixed points. He reaches out constantly toward a difficult, elusive beyond.

Of unequal lengths, the *Meditations* betray some design in numbers six, eleven and twelve where the development clearly appears to be more important. The *Eleventh* is unusual in the presentation of its second part; "Spirit" and "Soul" enter into a dialogue which provides a conclusion to the reflections presented by three personages, or personifications, "Intents," "Joints" and "Marrow." *Meditation Thirteen* likewise is a dialogue, between the Lord and the soul. These *Meditations* are less verbose than the others,

8. See note 6 above.

more rooted in a central idea, and manifestly allude to a particular stage in the life of the author. The *First Meditation* comes closer to these two in that it, too, is largely centred on a single theme. As for the *Twelfth*, it seems to be more philosophical in style. It is better worked out than the others, except perhaps for the *Sixth*.

In grouping these *Meditations*, William of St Thierry surely wished them to constitute a whole. He did not place them at random. But if the *Life* speaks of them as a treatise, it must be admitted that the treatise remains very much a composite.

Before beginning each *Meditation* it is best for the reader to consider the scriptural texts that William proposes for his prayer.[9] Actually, each *Meditation* is introduced by a Scriptural quotation. However this first text is not always its subject but instead only introduces it. The depths of God's wisdom presents to the spirit the mysteries of its ways, thus the Epistle to the Romans opens the *Meditations*. Other scriptural arguments follow one after another with the greatest of liberty. The psalmist invites William to come close to God in order to be illuminated (2), but a formidable objection presents itself—man cannot see God and live (3). God, however, is merciful (4). The *Fifth Meditation* cites no scriptural argument, but it can be considered a prolongation of the preceding, for it dwells somewhat at length on the Passion of Our Lord (5). At length William arrives at the open door of heaven while a voice cries out to him, "Come up here" (6). He does not enter, however, because we hear him saying to the Lord: "My face has sought your face" (7) to which comes the reply, "Show me your face" (8). Still one more reflection keeps William at a distance—the impious cannot see the glory of God (9). However, as he seeks his own glory only in the cross of Our Lord Jesus Christ (10), he pursues his quest, asking God to turn to him, show him his face (11), and grant his request (12).

A single contact with the *Meditations* provides an imperfect view,

---

9. The scriptural text is found eight times at the very beginning of the *Meditation*. Three times it comes after a few lines (2, 8, 9). Only one (5) is not based on a scriptural text. The numbers in parentheses refer to *Meditations*.

because the first impression is apt to be incomplete and sometimes inexact. The *Meditations* rarely limit their development to ideas connected with the initial text. The first one is about the only exception as it remains centered on the problems of human free will and divine prescience. *Meditation Thirteen* also follows the ideas expressed in the text "Come to me you who are in sorrow and I will refresh you." The other *Meditations* broach many themes which concatenate logically enough or which weave into one another in an artificial manner. The *Tenth* furnishes a simple example. After a quick mention of the cross, William speaks of the angels who help us in our desire to see the face of God. Then he treats of the "dispensation of the mystery of God," in order to consider eternal Wisdom and our effort at contemplation. He meditates rather at length on the Incarnation, makes a rapid reference to the unity of the Father and the Son, the role of the Holy Spirit and of the Eucharist in our union with God, and ends on the encounter between the face of God and the face of the creature. This summary, although it simplifies William's thought, permits a glimpse into the liberty of his prayer. It also shows the recurrence of themes already explored in other *Meditations*, for example, the Passion, the face of God.

In order to arrive at a better understanding of the subject of the *Meditations*, we should attempt a synthesis of the ideas that reappear most frequently. The central one is certainly that of a contemplation of the face of God. There is a tension here between two extremes, William and his misery—God and his infinite perfections—and it obliges the author to seek the means of bridging the abyss that separates them.[10]

Physical and moral misery, the weakness of nature itself, its powerlessness to attain to God, the cares of this present life, pastoral duties, the very imperfection of desire and of the effort toward God—all this overwhelms William who constantly bemoans his condition, his depravity (2, 5, 7, 8, 9, 11, 12, 13). He is a man of desire, but is his desire sincere? (2, 3, 8, 9). God himself adds to this unhappiness whenever he limits himself merely to passing by,

---

10. The following references are by no means exhaustive.

when his light serves only to cause the one who is rising to fall back again (2, 9, 11). For God is inaccessible in his nature and his majesty (3, 7) and also in his justice.

William, nevertheless, considers the divine Persons in the mystery of the Trinity (2, 3, 6, 7, 10). Among the means at his disposal for attaining to God, are the virtues of faith, hope, charity (1, 9, 11). He insists on the obscure knowledge of faith (2, 3). He loves to meditate on the mystery of Jesus—the model and the means—in his desire to be illumined (5, 6, 7, 8, 10, 11); willingly he dwells upon the Passion by which the Lord purifies him and pays his debt (3, 5, 8, 10, 12). If William speaks more than once of justice, of judgment (5, 6, 8, 9), it is in order to arrive at mercy and pardon (5, 8, 9, 11, 12). Once he has covered this road he will also speak of the Eucharist (8, 10). He sees Christ as the door of heaven, hence of contemplation (2, 5, 10, 11): the Holy Spirit as the bond in the Trinity, the author of our sanctification and union with God (2, 3, 4, 6, 8, 12). Yet he does not neglect the help obtained for us by the blessed and the angels (2, 6, 7, 10, 12).

Other notions reappear frequently. Noteworthy are the passages where William refers to the place of God (3, 6, 10). The definition he gives of the will and its degrees (especially 12), is very striking. The word "facing" might be used to characterize the *Meditations*, whether in regard to God or man or the encounter between the two (3, 7, 8, etc.). But the word "image" comes still more often from William's pen (3, 7, 11, 12), so attentive is he to the restoration in man of the divine image (3, 4, 5, 6) and to God's indwelling which enlightens man (2, 12) and make him like God (6).

We will not discuss here the question of sources, nevertheless, it can be noted how much Gregory has nourished the mind and the heart of the Abbot of St Thierry.

Whether developed in some degree, or merely mentioned in passing, the themes that have been singled out provide the principal nourishment to William's prayer. The most elaborate, and at the same time the most rich in thought, are certainly *Meditations Six* and *Twelve*, both of which contain a doctrine of vision through love. Having made this remark, one might be tempted to divide the

Meditations into two series of six, but such a division does not stand examination. To constitute a coherent ensemble, it would be necessary to visualize the *First Meditation* as an introduction, the last as a conclusion. Between the two we would have two series of five. Actually, *Seven* corresponds to *Two* on the desire for the face of God; *Five* to *Ten* on the Passion theme. There would be a certain rapport between *Four* when William speaks of divine mercy and *Nine* where he undertakes an examination of conscience. In *Meditations Three* and *Eight* we encounter the idea that the sinner cannot see God, but that God reveals himself to the soul of good will and transforms it. While contrasting the beatitude of the elect in heaven with the misery of the Abbot of St Thierry on earth, *Meditations Six* and *Eleven* firmly establish happiness as being in contemplation of the vision of God.

But is such an attempt at systematization valid? Would this not be to simplify William's reflection wrongly? Far too much of a thinker not to steer his thought along the course of a few dominant ideas, William, nevertheless, never pretends to propose to the reader a methodical exposition, but rather, to habituate him to the search for God in prayer.

Scholars have endeavored to assign a date to the *Meditations*. Noting a few expressions which seemed characteristic of a certain moment in William's life, and applying to the ensemble of the book what they found in only one of the *Meditations*, they isolated expressions from their context and even from the sentence in which they were found. Thus they arrived at conclusions which were hardly results that were in accord, placing the redaction of the *Meditations* now at St Thierry, now at Signy.

Manrique[11] proposed Signy because William declares: "I gave nothing to the poor since I possessed nothing" (11:3). If he is alluding to himself in the passage where this assertion is found, it is far more likely that it concerns his entrance into the monastic life. William continues, saying that he can go no further, which might be

---

11. Angelo Manrique, *Cisterciensium seu Verius Ecclesiasticorum Annalium a Condito Cistercio*, Lyon, 1642, vol. I, p. 282.

understood as referring to the impossibility of leaving St Thierry.
But are all these texts really designed to recount a life? Or do they
rather attempt to define a spiritual itinerary?

Tissier[12] follows Manrique, adding an allusion to the flight into
solitude (4) without taking into account that it is not a question here
of advance in the spiritual life, but rather of a repentant sinner who
is still not able to master himself.

Again Manrique points out, in a passage that is characteristic
enough, an opposition between the former abbatial position and
the humility of the present condition: "As once I took pleasure in
being in authority, so now my will is to be in subjection" (11:16).
However, this is to anticipate because this *Meditation* which can be
most easily situated in William's life, is a long lament on the labors
of the abbacy, on the impossibility of recovering unity and peace.[13]

Abbé Adam[14] places the *Meditations* during the abbacy at St
Thierry and bases himself on the *Ninth Meditation*. There, William
does describe his misery in his development on the obstacles to
contemplation, but there is nothing to indicate a special period in
his life.

Is Dom J. M. Déchanet any more correct when, in summarizing
the researches of his predecessors, he concludes that the *Meditations*,
sections of which might have been prepared at various times, were
collected together into one whole at Signy between 1135 and 1145?

It cannot be denied that William did not draft these at one
sitting. Anyone familiar with William's working methods knows
that this, even more than other works, could not have been done in
a single breath. He is the man of renewed reflections, of arduous
research. He takes notes, he makes dossiers, he assembles his material
by stages. Little by little he makes his thinking more precise and

12. PL 180:215. Dom Déchanet in *William of St Thierry, The Man and his
Work* (Cistercian Studies Series 10) agrees with Tissier. He sees in the *Fourth
Meditation* sure allusions to health problems that mark the beginning of the
sojourn at Signy.

13. The term *praesse* characterizes well the condition of the abbot (cf. *The
Rule of St Benedict*, 2; 5; 64), but William's desire is not yet realized.

14. A. Adam, *Guillaume de Saint-Thierry* (Bourg, 1923), p. 53.

progressively sets it in order. Analysis of the *Meditations* and comparison with other writings allow one to isolate a considerable number of parts which have been gathered into small units, and then combined to form one whole.

It remains then to discover when this was done. Two clues point to the abbacy at St Thierry. The first, an entirely material one, is the presence of the *Meditations* in the Reuil manuscript as an introduction to the two treatises *On Contemplating God* and on *The Nature and Dignity of Love*. William's reference to them in his covering letter to the brethren of Mont-Dieu confirms this hypothesis. A second clue, and a more telling one, is William's thought in this writing. In the order of the Reuil manuscript, we have three treatises, progressively less affective, better ordered. Even if William kept the material for the *Meditations* filed while he was writing the two later works, these notes represent the initial stage of his study. He would have arranged them in order, if not in form, at the time he gave the three texts to the copyist, who made a sort of triptych of them.

The opening *Meditation*, centred on the problem of justification, contrasts to some degree with the rest of the work in that only with difficulty does one find here the themes that are developed further on. If William leaves it this way, may it not be because he attributes some particular importance to it? This would be the moment when preoccupied with the problem of grace, he is compiling the commentaries on the Epistle to the Romans,[15] and asking light of Bernard who will reply with the treatise, *On Grace and Free Will*.[16] The year 1128, in which this last work is placed, furnishes a chronological guide.[17] The reflections of *Meditation Eleven* indicate a weary abbot, anxious to be rid of the crozier. Yet, it is all but impossible to determine when he let himself be so carried away by his pessimism

---

15. *Expositio in Epistolam ad Romanos* (PL 180:547).

16. *The Works of Bernard of Clairvaux*, vol. 7 (Cistercian Fathers Series 19).

17. Father Jean de la Croix Bouton, in the collection *Bernard de Clairvaux* (Paris, 1953), p. 237, intimates this date. In 1130 *On Grace and Free Will* is known and used in the Premonstratensian Order (Dom François Petit: *ibid.* p. 306).

before the flight to Signy in 1135. Thus we might propose that around 1128–1132, William of St Thierry, who has already written his two books on the love of God, adds to them a collection of prayers most of which are anterior to this time. Thus, he constitutes a succession of treatises whose common subject is contemplation by love.

Very personal, both as to content and form, the *Meditations* reveal William's prayer even while giving instruction in prayer. They are cast in a style then in honor. In the wake of St Augustine, the literature of the *Soliloquies* and the *Meditations* can count many celebrated names such as Anselm, John of Fécamp, Hugh of Victor, and others, thinkers of great breadth and men of heart, who enriched monastic spirituality in a way that is proper to it. William of St Thierry takes his place with them, bringing a warmth which is all the more original because of his personal theological orientation.

The three treatises of the Reuil manuscript allow us to follow the progress of a thought that reveals the method of the abbot. A prayer, rich in philosophical and theological ideas, leads on to more scientific thinking by struggling toward a better ordered though not purely systematic exposition and the more scientific exposition continues to bear the traits of an ardent prayer. Some fundamental ideas stand out: the relationship between love and knowledge and the increase of this knowledge—love in the three stages of the spiritual life of man—the animal, the rational, the spiritual. Indeed, the purpose of the *Meditations* is to draw us into William's labor of love and understanding.

Jacques Hourlier OSB

HERE BEGIN
THE MEDITATIONS[1]
OF
DOM WILLIAM
ABBOT OF ST THIERRY

MEDITATION ONE

*The foreknowledge of God, and
the mystery of predestination and of reprobation.*[2]

"OTHE DEPTH OF THE WISDOM and knowledge of God! How unsearchable are his judgments and his ways are past finding out! For who has known the mind of the Lord, or who has been his counsellor?"[3] For you have mercy, Lord, on whom you will have mercy; you have pity on whom you will have pity. Election "is not of him who wills, nor of him who runs, but of God who shows mercy."[4]

2. The earthen vessel recoils from the hand of him who made it, of him who says by the Prophet: "I have made, and I will bear."[5] Deserving of destruction as it is, fit to be crushed and broken, it breaks away from the hand that carries it and cries: "Why does he then find fault? For who resists his will?"[6] And it continues: "Why have you made me thus?"[7]

That, O eternal Wisdom, is how the earthen vessel speaks to you! Thus speaks the pot of clay, the vessel of reproach and wrath, made

---

1. *Meditativae orationes*—this is the collective title found in the Mazarine ms.

2. The subtitles are taken from the edition M. M. Davy and are not in the ms. They probably originated with Tissier.

3. Rom 11:33f. What follows is based on Rom 9:16–23. In verse 19: *quid adhuc quaeritur?* means rather: "What more does he want?" The Douay version: "Why doth he find fault?" presupposes *queritur* (from the deponent *queror*) in the place of *quaeritur*, and that is what the Greek, Τί ἔτι μέμφεται, requires. For the figure of the potter and the clay, see Jer 18:1ff.

4. Rom 9:15f.   5. Is 46:4.
6. Rom 9:19.   7. Rom 9:20.

for perdition,[8] when it behoves it rather to tremble before you and to pray to you who, out of the selfsame lump, have power to make one vessel for an honorable use, another for reproach.[9] But the chosen vessels, those that are made for honor, they endure. They are the vessels of mercy prepared by you for your glory; and they do not speak like that, but rather they acknowledge you as their creator and their potter, and themselves clay to which your hand has given form. And woe betide them if they fall away from your hand, for then they will be broken and crushed and reduced to nothing! They know this, and do not forsake your grace.

3. Have mercy on us, Lord, have mercy! You are our potter and we are the clay. Somehow or other, we have held together until now; we are still carried by your mighty hand, and we are still clinging to your three fingers, faith, hope and charity, with which you support the whole great bulk of earth—that is to say, the whole weight of your holy Church.[10] Cleanse our reins and our hearts[11] by the fire of your Holy Spirit, and establish the work that you have wrought in us,[12] lest we be loosed asunder and return again to clay or nothingness. We were created for you by yourself, and towards you our face is set.[13] We acknowledge you our maker and creator; we adore your wisdom and pray that it may order all our life. We adore your goodness and mercy, and beg them ever to sustain and help us. You who have made us, bring us to perfection; perfect in us the image and likeness of yourself for which you made us.

4. The earthen vessel destined to return to earth demands of you

8. Rom 9:22.   9. Rom 9:21.   10. Is 40:12.

11. Ps 25:2.   12. Ps 67:29.

13. Song 7:10. See Gen 1:26. In the course of these *Meditations* William will frequently return to the Augustinian doctrine of man created *ad imaginem*—to the image of God. Deformed by sin the image is reformed by grace. See Augustine, *Enarr. in Psalmos*, 4, 6 (PL 36:480); *De Trinitate*, 14 (PL 42:1096f.). The Cistercian and Carthusian authors of the twelfth century frequently take up this theory following William of St Thierry and St Bernard. However there does seem to be a real difference in the way William and Bernard treat this theme. For William the image itself is lost by sin, while for Bernard the image always remains even in the soul of the damned, while the likeness is what is lost.

with the voice of one falling and remonstrating: "Why have you made me thus?"[14] But the vessel made for honor does not address you so, for it believes with the heart unto righteousness and confesses with the mouth unto salvation[15] that you are good, and have done all things well.[16] Even in making one for honor and another for reproach you have done well, in that you have bestowed free will on both, so that each, acting as he does not of necessity but of his own deliberate choice, should have the degree of merit proper to the virtue he displays. For virtue is precisely the deliberate assent of the good will to what is good.[17]

5. But, O eternal Wisdom, since you know everything, you know beforehand concerning both how they would use that freedom of will, and how they would decide their destiny; and you were ready to bestow your grace on one as on the other, if only he would not receive that grace in vain.[18] Yet your foreknowledge in no way forces them to be what they will severally be, as though their future were determined by the fact of your foreknowing it; rather, you know beforehand that they will be so, because they will be so, and therefore you, who know everything before it comes to pass, know this too, and your foreknowledge can make no mistakes. Moreover, your foreknowledge, O my God, is one thing with your wisdom, which is with you from all eternity, and so would it have been with you, had never a creature existed. In it is the eternal ground of all that happens in time, and by that same foreknowledge all creatures come to be in their own time. And yet creation was never in the future in regard to you, for life was in your consubstantial Word, who made all that was made.[19] In him was life,[20] as it was to be in the future, exactly as it was to be, because life was in

14. Rom 9:20.   15. Rom 10:10.   16. Mk 7:37.

17. In this *Meditation* one senses a certain give and take. Up to this point the accent has been placed on the power of the divine predestination dominating human liberty and one perceives the influence of St Augustine. From here on the accent is placed on the divine foreknowledge contenting itself to consider the freedom of man in his operation, and it seems we may have here a certain influence of the Greek Fathers. See the note of Dom Déchanet at the end of the first *Meditation* in *Meditations et Prières* (Brussels, 1954), pp. 95ff.

18. 2 Cor 6:1.   19. Jn 1:3.   20. Jn 1:4.

G

him. But that life did not force it so to be; it existed thus in him, because it would be so.

6. What then? Does the temporal form of the future determine the Being of God, his very eternity? For it seems that, if the future were not to be cast in this mold, it could not exist eternally in the Word of God. But your knowledge, O God, and your fore-knowledge are your truth that says: "I am the truth."[21] And as you by foreknowing do not constrain the future to be such as you fore-know, so can you not yourself be forced to foreknow anything by the mere fact of its futurity. There is no past with you, nor future either; but you are ever what you are, and all that exists in any mode whatever, be it past, or present, or future, is alive in your Word.

7. "The wicked walk round in a circle."[22] Remove yourself, O man, away from the circumference of error to the center of truth! When the earthen vessel turns to clay again, it does so under no compulsion from the fact that God foreknew it would do so, and that its future was not hidden from him; and yet, because God knew that this would happen, he foreordained it to destruction.

8. God's foreknowledge is the same thing as his goodness, which he is eternally ready to bestow on all, although not all are ready to accept it. Who will accept, and who will not, this also is within the field of God's foreknowledge which, if it be equated with his good-ness as I said just now, was ready for all from all eternity, even had nothing ever been created. For this goodness is the Holy Spirit, co-eternal with the Father and the Son. Wherefore it is written that, at the creation of the world the Spirit moved upon the waters[23]—that is to say, he was offering himself to all and showing himself to them by doing and providing things needful for their use, as it is his function to do; but at the same time he was fleeing from the soul that was ill-disposed, into which wisdom can effect no entrance.[24]

9. Foreknowledge concerning things created, therefore, is foreknowledge on the part of God; but, when viewed in regard to

21. Jn 14:6.   22. Ps 11:9.   23. Gen 1:2.

24. Wis 1:4. This whole passage concerning the Holy Spirit is penetrated with the doctrine of Augustine. See in particular, *In Joan.*, 98, 3 ; (PL 35:1881); *Contra Serm. Arian.*, 32 (PL 42:715).

men, it is predestination, which term includes election and reprobation equally. That is why he tells us: "You have not chosen me, but
I have chosen you."[25] Predestination is at once the preparation for
grace and the result of it. And why one should be taken into grace
and another rejected, is a question you had best not ask, unless you
wish to go astray.[26] If you are proud, the fact of your pride is no
secret from God, and you do not escape the providence by which he
has foreordained you to the punishment made ready for proud
men. "For God resists the proud, but gives grace to the humble."[27]
Pride, therefore, is at once the thing that merits reprobation and the
sign of it just as humility is that which both deserves election and
denotes it.

10. If, then, the earthen vessel says: "Why have you made me
thus?"—that is to say: "Why have you foreordained me to destruction?"—the Truth will answer: "To speak in your own terms, it
was because I knew beforehand that you would be a vessel of wrath
meet for destruction, a fool who neither knew salvation nor desired
it, a soul so proud that you would scorn humiliation. Because I knew
all that, I lodge no further complaint, but you will go irrevocably
to destruction. You do not stay the operation of my will, since my
will is that my mercy should be very near the wretched—to those,
that is to say, who knew their wretchedness—but that those who
are mighty in iniquity should suffer mighty pains.[28] Only on the
humble will I show my pity; it is on the merciful that I have
mercy.[29] So do not keep on asking me: 'Why did you not give me

---

25. Jn 15:16.

26. Again it is the mystery of predestination seen from the Augustinian
point of view; the two formulas are taken almost verbally from St Augustine:
"The predestination of God in regard to the good is the preparation of grace;
grace itself is an effect of predestination."—*De Praed. Sanctorum*, 19. "No one
comes unless he is drawn. Whom he draws and whom he does not draw, why
he draws one and does not draw another—do not wish to judge if you do not
wish to err."—*In Joan.*, 26, 2.

27. Jas 4:6.

28. Ps 51:3; Wis 6:7.

29. Ex 33:19 as it is cited in Rom 9:15.

humility?' I gave you a greater gift than that—free will. And you have grown mighty in iniquity by the use of that very gift; you have loved malice more than kindness.[30] What is more, you have tried to make me responsible for your bad deeds; for so determined are you to excuse yourself that you have laid the blame for them on me! You refuse to admit the hatefulness of your iniquity;[31] therefore you shall go to your own place,[32] vessel of wrath that you are, and meet to be destroyed!"

30. Ps 51:5.   31. Ps 35:3.   32. Acts 1:25.

*William presents himself to God, desiring to receive his
light and, with a mind detached from things of sense, to
meditate upon the Holy Trinity.*

"COME UNTO HIM and be enlightened, and your
faces shall not be ashamed."[1] But I am ashamed, O Lord,
and confounded with a hideous and terrible confusion, as
often as I come to you and find the door of vision shut. Almost I
seem to hear the fearful words: "Truly I tell you, I do not know
you."[2] I desired that you should enlighten me, and now my grief
of heart and sore perplexity have thrown me into darkness so
complete that it almost seems it had been better for me if I had not
come.

2. For where shall I seek comfort, if desolation is your will for me?
Away with every consolation that neither is yourself nor comes
from you! May they perish! "Woe to him who is alone,"[3] says
Solomon. Woe indeed to me if I be alone, if you are not with me,
nor yet I with you!

I reckon myself blessed, Lord, and highly blessed, if I feel you
with me; but I am wearisome and hateful to myself whenever I

1. Ps 33:6.   2. Mt 25:12.

3. Eccles 4:10. William of St Thierry who is more eremitically inclined (see
below, *Meditation Four*, 9, p. 115, applies this text to his relation with God. But
the Cistercian Fathers in general understood it more commonly according to
its literal sense, applying it to the horizontal relations within the community
life. See e.g., Guerric of Igny, *Fourth Sermon for Advent*, 2; trans. T. Berkeley,
The Liturgical Sermons of Guerric of Igny I (Cistercian Fathers Series 8), pp. 23f.;
Bernard of Clairvaux, *On the Song of Songs*, 33:10; trans. K. Walsh, *The
Works of Bernard of Clairvaux*, vol. 3 (Cistercian Fathers Series 7).

perceive that I am not with you. As long as I am with you, I am
also with myself; I am no longer myself when I am not with you.
And woe is me whenever I am not with you, for no existence is
possible for me apart from you. I could not exist in any way at all,
either in body or in soul, save by your constant power, I could not
desire you, nor seek you save by your ever present grace; and I
could never find you, did not your mercy and your goodness run
to meet me on my way. In all these things I am with you, and I am
conscious of your grace at work in me; the fact that I exist and am
alive seems good to me; my soul makes her boast in the Lord.[4] But
if, when you are present in thus doing good to me, I am myself
absent from you in mind and heart, the operations of your grace, it
seems to me, are like burial rites duly and carefully fulfilled upon a
corpse.

3. Sometimes I feel you passing by, you do not stop for me but go
straight on, leaving me crying after you like the Canaanite woman.[5]
And when you weary of the crying with which my misery impor-
tunes you, speaking as to a dog you reproach my sullied conscience
with its past impurity and present shame; and you drive your dog
from your table unfed and famished and beaten by the rebukes of
his conscience, or you just let him go. Should I draw near again,
when this occurs? Yes, surely, Lord. For the whelps that are chased
with blows from their master's house return immediately and,
hanging watchfully about the place, receive their daily bread. I
come again when I am driven out; shut out, I howl; and beaten, I
implore. A dog cannot live without a man's companionship, nor
can my soul without the Lord her God.

4. Open to me, therefore, Lord, that I may come to you and be
enlightened by you. You dwell in your heavens,[6] but you have
made darkness your secret place, even the dark waters amid the
clouds of the air.[7] And, as the Prophet says, "You have set a cloud
before you, so that our prayer may not pass through."[8]

But, as for me, I have rotted on earth,[9] I have made the thick and

4. Ps 33:3.   5. Mt 15:21ff.; Mk 7:24ff.   6. Ps 122:1.
7. Ps 17:12.   8. Lam 3:44.   9. Ex 8:14.

earthy covering of my heart more heavy even than it was before.[10] Your heavenly stars do not shine for me; the sun is darkened[11] and the moon gives no light.[12] In psalms and hymns and spiritual songs[13] I hear your mighty acts proclaimed; out of your Gospels your words and deeds shine forth at me, and the example of your servants strikes unceasingly upon my eyes and ears. Your promises in Scripture, the promises your Truth has made, obtruding themselves without cease upon my sight and battering my deafness with their din, shake me with fears and taunt me. But long persistence in bad ways, along with very great insensibility of mind,[14] has hardened me. I have learned to sleep with the sunshine full on my face, and have grown used to it. I have become accustomed to not seeing what takes place before my eyes and, dead at heart as I am,[15] though I am set in the midst of the sea, I have ceased to hear the roaring of its waves and the thunder of the sky.

5. How long, O Lord, how long? How long will you defer to rend the heavens and come down?[16] How long will you delay to fulfill your wrath upon me, and so to shatter my dullness that I may be no longer what I am, but may know that it is you who rules Jacob and the utmost bounds of earth, and so be turned, at least at eventide, and hunger like a dog that runs about your city[17]—your city of which a portion sojourns still on earth but the greater part rejoices already in heaven—so that maybe I may find some who will receive my fainting soul into their habitation,[18] my soul that has no couch of her own on which to lay her head?[19]

6. Sometimes indeed I hear your Spirit's voice, and, though it is no more than as the whistling of a gentle air[20] that passes me, I understand the message: "*Come unto him and be enlightened.*"[21] I hear, and I am shaken. Arising as from sleep and shaking off my lethargy, a certain wonder fills me. I open my mouth and I draw in my

---

10. Hab 2:6; Lam 3:65.

11. Lk 23:45; Rev. 9:2.

12. Mt 24:29.   13. Eph 5:19.

14. Acts 22:17.

15. Ps 30:13.   16. Ps 12:1; Is 6:11; 64:1.

17. Ps 58:14f.

18. Lk 16:9.   19. Mt 8:20.

20. 1 Kings 19:11f.

21. Ps 33:6.

breath;[22] I stretch my spiritual muscles and rouse them from their sloth. I turn my back on the shades of night in which my conscience lies and come forth to the Sun of Righteousness who is rising now for me. But I am drowsy still, and the eyes of my reason are dazzled when I try to look at him. For they are used to darkness and unaccustomed to the light; and, while both pupils and eyelids tremble and blink at the unwonted brightness, as best I can I wipe the rheum of my long sleep from them with the hand of exercise.[23] If by your gift I find a fount of tears[24] such as is wont to spring up speedily in lowly ground and in the valleys of a contrite soul, I wash the hands with which I work and the face I lift in prayer. Then, as the falcon spreads his wings towards the south to make his feathers grow,[25] I stretch out my two hands to you, O Lord. My soul is as waterless ground in your sight,[26] and as desert land, unwatered and untrodden, I appear before you in your holy place, that I may see your power and your glory.[27] And when I raise to you, O Sun of Righteousness, the eyes of my mind and the perception of my reason, it happens to me as is wont to happen to persons drunk with sleep or of weak eyes. Seeing one thing, they think that they are seeing two or three, until in the process of seeing it dawns upon them that the defect is in their sight, and not in the thing seen. For when my soul, that has been used to find her pleasure through the senses and in things that they can apprehend, is roused from these preoccupations, she is forthwith confronted with a mental picture that baffles her with images derived from things of sense. Her powers of perception have been blunted by her former exclusive attention to things sensible, with the result that now she does not

---

22. Ps 118:131.

23. William here again points out the role of action—the exercise of the virtues—in preparation for contemplation. See also, *On the Nature and Dignity of Love*, 8ff.; trans. J. T. Cummings, *The Works of William of St Thierry*, vol. 5 (Cistercian Fathers Series 15); *Exposition on the Song of Songs*, 198; *op. cit.*, pp. 159f. In this he is in complete agreement with Bernard of Clairvaux, *On the Song of Songs*, 47:4 (Cistercian Fathers Series 7).

24. Jer 9:1.   25. Job 39:26.

26. Ps 142:6.   27. Ps 62:3.

know how to apprehend or think of anything except under such forms.[28]

7. For this reason, therefore, when on awaking from the sleep of negligence I suddenly direct my gaze on God, concerning whom the divine law instructs me, saying: "Hear, O Israel! The Lord your God is one God,"[29] and while I fix my soul's regard entirely on him from whom I look for light and whom I am about to worship or implore, I am confronted with the fact of God as Trinity. This mystery the catholic faith, rehearsed by my forebears, impressed upon me by long use, and commended to me by yourself and those who teach your truth, declares to me. But my soul's foolish way of picturing things sees and regards the Trinity in such a fashion, that she fondly thinks that there is number in the simple Being of the Godhead which, itself beyond all number, made all that is by number and by measure and by weight.[30] And she thinks of the several Persons of the Trinity as having each his place, and prays to the Father, through the Son, and in the Holy Spirit, as though she passed from one to the other through the third. And so my mind, befogged by the one, is scattered between the three, just as if there were three bodies to be differentiated or to be made one.

8. When the imagination—that is to say, the mind that thus envisages the Trinity, does so in spite of itself or suffers that mode of thought unwillingly and under protest, faith comes in and censures it. Reason through faith gives judgment; authority condemns, and all that is within me cries out[31] likewise what was said before: "Hear, O Israel! The Lord your God is one God."[32] For, although faith, reason and authority alike all teach me to think of the Father, the Son, and the Spirit each by himself, they will allow no element

28. William here touches upon one of his favorite themes which is to some extent inspired by neoplatonic philosophy. When the soul is detached from sensible things it receives the divine illumination. On the contrary when it is bound to the sensible it cannot free itself from the images coming from the senses (See e.g., *Golden Epistle*, 62ff.). The passage which follows, pointing out the difficulty imagination causes in contemplation of the Trinity, has a close parallel in the *Enigma of Faith*, nn. 12f., *The Works of William of St Thierry*, vol. 3 (Cistercian Fathers Series 9).

29. Deut 6:4.   30. Wis 11:21.   31. Ps 102:1.   32. Deut 6:4.

whatever in my thought of the Trinity, which either suggests division of its substance in time or place or number, or seems to imply confusion of the Persons. They so assert the unity of the Trinity as to rule out solitude; and the threefoldness of the Unity they so declare as to exclude from the Being of God plurality of number. Your grace, O Lord, which precedes everything of worth in us, every capacity or skill or virtue, gives us some little knowledge of ourselves and you. And grace submits us to humility, humility to authority, authority to faith; faith teaches reason; reason, by means of faith, either refines the picture that the mind has formed, or else destroys it and supplies another. Reason, however, does not teach faith in order to bring it to understanding; rather, through faith it looks for understanding to come down from above, from you, the Father of lights, from whom is every good and perfect gift.[33] And the understanding which is not derived from reason, nor reached by process of thought, but comes from the throne of your greatness[34] as the reward of faith and is determined by your wisdom—that understanding is altogether like the fountain whence it springs. For, entering the mind of the believer, it takes reason to itself and makes it like itself; by it faith also is imbued with life and light.[35]

9. The soul about to pray to you, her God, stands therefore frightened and bewildered, holding herself in her hands all the time,[36] that she may make herself an offering to you. Fearful of that to which she has been used, and dazed by things unwonted, she bears the signet of your faith with which to find you, but so far has not found the wax to yield to its impression. She seeks your face, O Lord, she seeks your face,[37] not knowing, yet not wholly ignorant

---

33. Jas 1:17.   34. Wis 9:10.

35. A good and original presentation of the action of understanding, that understanding that comes from God and which adds to faith if not certainty at least understanding and insight.

36. Ps 118:109.

37. Ps 26:8. A favorite text of William; see below *Meditations* 3:3; 7:1ff.; 8:5. William was fascinated by the "face of God." He returns to it again and again in the course of these *Meditations*, where he draws his inspiration from

of what she seeks. The phantoms of her heart concerning you she hates as idols. She loves you as her faith presents you to her, but her mind fails to win the sight of you. Aflame with longing for your face, before which she would offer her sacrifice of righteousness and duty, her oblations and burnt offerings,[38] she is more troubled when she is put off. And when for all her asking she still fails to win the light of faith from you in whom she trusted, she sometimes grows so disconcerted that she can hardly believe she does believe in you at all, and she hates herself because it seems to her she has no love for you! But far be it from her, who is so anguished by desire for you, that she should not believe in you, or that she should not love you who desires you to the exclusion of all things that are and even of herself!

10. How long, O Lord, how long?[39] If you do not light my candle, if you do not illuminate my darknesses, I shall not be delivered from these straits. Nor, save by you, my God, shall I surmount this wall.[40]

---

the Scriptures: Ps 15:11, the joy of his face: *Med.* 3:2, 6:2, 7:5; Ps 88:16, walking in the light of his face: *Med.* 3:3, 7:5; Ps 16:2, the face guiding his judgment: *Med.* 3:3, 7:5; Ps 30:21, hiding in the hidden recesses of his face: *Med.* 4:11, 9:5, 11:2; Ps 4:7, in the light of his face: *Med.* 8:1, 9:6. Many other references to this face are to be found in these *Meditations*, e.g., 10:8, 11:1, 12:5, and in William's other works—see *Exposition on the Song of Songs, op. cit.*, pp. 28f., note 17.

38. Ps 50:21.   39. Ps 12:1.   40. Ps 17:29f.

MEDITATION THREE

William gives utterance to his longing to see God,
and dwells on the joy of that sight.

I DARE NOT NOW, Lord, look upon your face, for all
that I desire it even unto death, for you said to Moses," There
shall no man see me, and live."[1] I do indeed desire to die that
I may see, or see that I may die; and yet I hide my face, as Moses
did, not venturing to meet you eye to eye. For so it is there written,
"And Moses hid his face, for he dared not look upon the Lord."[2]
He would have looked upon the Lord, perhaps, if he had tried to
see, not who God is, but what.[3] For who God is he had already
heard; "I am the God of Abraham," God said, "the God of Isaac,
and the God of Jacob."[4]

2. And yet to this same Moses who, on hearing that his death was
near, was all aflame with this selfsame desire and prayed that you
would let him see your glory, you replied, "I will show you All
Good."[5] And where, Lord, is All Good, save in your face? That is
why David, burning with the same desire, says, "You shall fill me
with joy from your face."[6]

3. Forgive me, Lord, forgive my heart's impatience for you; I
seek your face,[7] by your own gift I seek your countenance, lest you
should turn it from me at the last.[8]

1. Ex 33:20.   2. Ex 3:6.

3. "Who God is"—that is to inquire of God as one might inquire of a person
what might be his name, but "what" is to seek to know the depths of God,
his intimate nature.

4. Ex 3:6.

5. Ex 33:19.   6. Ps 15:11.   7. Ps 26:8.   8. Ps 26:9.

I know indeed and I am sure[9] that those who walk in the light of your countenance[10] do not fall but walk in safety, and by your face their every judgment is directed.[11] They are the living people, for their life is lived according to that which they read and see in your face, as in an exemplar. O Lord, I dare not look upon your face against your will, lest I be further confounded. Needy and beggared and blind,[12] I stand in your presence, seen by you though I do not see you. And, standing thus, I offer you my heart full of desire for you, the whole of whatever I am, the whole of whatever I can do, the whole of whatever I know, and the very fact that I so yearn and faint for you. But the way to find you, that I do not find.

4. Where are you, Lord, where are you? And where, Lord, are you not? This much at least I know, and that most certainly,[13] that you, in whom we move and have our being,[14] are in a manner present here with me, and that from that most healthgiving presence comes the longing and fainting of my soul for your salvation.[15] I know in very truth, I am aware most healthfully, that you are with me. I know, I feel, I worship, and I render thanks. But, if you are with me, why am I not with you? What hinders it? What is the obstacle? What gets in the way? If you are with me, working for my good, why am I not in the same way with you, enjoying you, the supreme Good of all? Is it because of my sins? But where is he who took them out of the way and nailed them to his cross?[16] And surely it is not because I do not love him! Would I not die a hundred and a thousand times for you, Lord Jesus? If this is not enough for you, no more is it for me; for nothing satisfies my soul, nor does she seem to herself to love you at all, if she has no joy of you. But she cannot so enjoy you, until you grant her to see and know you after her own manner.

But why does she not see you? As I now love you even unto

9. 2 Tim 1:12.   10. Ps 88:16.

11. Ps 16:2. We can see in this passage William's preoccupation, when inspired by the Psalms, with the face of God. This reoccurs frequently in his writings; see above *Med.* 2, note 37.

12. Rev 3:17; Lk 18:35.   13. 2 Tim 1:12.   14. Acts 17:28.

15. Ps 18:81.   16. Col 2:14.

death, so would I love unto eternal life. Already, Lord, some of your nameless fragrance reaches me; if I could only sense it perfectly, henceforward I should search no more. You do indeed send me at times as it were mouthfuls of your consolation; but what is that for hunger such as mine? O you, Salvation of my soul,[17] tell her, please tell her, why you have inbreathed this longing into her; surely it is not merely to torment and rend and slay! And yet, if only it would slay! Lord, I implore you: is this then my hell? Very well, so be it! Go on putting me to torture ceaselessly, and, in that hell, let me burn ceaselessly, knowing no respite from its pains one single day, or hour, or moment even, till I appear before your presence[18] and behold your glory,[19] and the eternal feast day of your face has shone upon my soul!

5. When Moses, Lord, of old covered his countenance and veiled his face before you,[20] he symbolized the people under his command, who were for ever fleeing from the face of God. But Paul, your Paul, who is all ours because he is all yours, the clarion voice of the New Testament,[21] says of himself and his followers in your desire and love: "We all with unveiled face beholding the glory of the Lord are changed into the same image from glory to glory."[22]

That man of yours was fleeing to your face, and not away from it.[23]

6. Forgive, O Lord, forgive my boldness and my importunity; we dare so much, only because we are consumed with longing,[24] because your fire drives us, which you came to send on earth, and which you longed so greatly to see enkindled.[25] By your almightiest goodness, Lord, I pray you, by your most tender patience towards us, yield something to my quest, and tell my soul what she desires

---

17. Ps 34:3.   18. Ps 41:3; Deut 31:11.

19. Lev 9:6; Num 14:10; 16:19; 20:6; Ps 16:15.

20. Ex 34:33f.; 2 Cor 3:13, 15.

21. William here deliberately contrasts the term covenants or testatments when he speaks first of "Moses of old"—*vetus ille Moyses*—and then of Paul "the clarion voice of the New Testament"—*Novi Testamenti tuba.*

22. 2 Cor 3:18.   23. Ps 67:2.

24. *Audemus, quia ardemus.*   25. Lk 12:49.

when she seeks your face. For so purblind is she, so vexed within herself, that she is growing feeble even in her longing, and does not know just what it is she longs for. Does she desire to see you as you are?[26] And what does "as" mean there? Does it mean "of what sort"? Or "how great"? But you, O Lord, are not of any "sort" nor have you measure; there is no quality nor quantity in you, who are what you are. So, "as you are," what does it mean? It is beyond our powers so to see you, for to see what you are is to be what you are. And no man sees the Father but the Son, neither does any see the Son except the Father;[27] for this is to be the Father—to see the Son, and this is to be the Son—to see the Father. But the Lord adds, "and he to whomsoever the Son shall have willed to reveal him."[28] Now the Father and the Son have not two wills, but one, which is the Holy Spirit. Through the Holy Spirit, therefore, the Triune God reveals himself to any friend of God on whom he would bestow especial honor.[29] But does man ever see God as the Father sees the Son, or the Son the Father, who see each other as we said in such wise as to be not separate but one God? Yes, assuredly, but not in every way the same.

7. To make this somewhat clearer, let us consider the physical faculty of sight and the power of apprehension that pertains to it. Every bodily sense, in order to be a sense and to perceive at all, must be in some sort changed, by means of a certain sensible impression, into the thing perceived: sight, that is to say, must be changed into that which it sees, hearing into that which is heard, and so with all the rest. Otherwise it does not perceive and it is not a sense. The sense, then, is no sense, neither can it perceive at all unless, when it has informed the reason of the thing perceived, the soul of the perceiver is changed by a certain transformation of itself into the reality perceived, or into its state.[30] If, therefore, it

26. 1 Jn 3:2. The words of St John: "We will see him as he is" refer to the Beatific Vision.

27. Mt 11:27.   28. *Ibid.*   29. Esther 6:6, 9.

30. William develops the same theory of sensation in his *Exposition on the Song of Songs*, n. 100. (Cistercian Fathers Series 6), pp. 80f. and in his *Mirror of Faith*, n. 27 (Cistercian Fathers Series 9).

perceives that God is good, by means of love which is its proper sense, and loves him for his goodness, it must inevitably be made good itself in being thus joined to God by a good disposition.

8. To return to the sense of the soul,[31] is it not of this that Paul is speaking when he says: "Beholding the glory of God, we are changed into the same image"?[32] That is how the soul's sense functions. For the soul's sense is love; by love it perceives whatever it perceives, alike when it is pleased and when it is offended. When the soul reaches out in love to anything, a certain change takes place in it by which it is transmuted into the object loved; it does not become of the same nature as that object, but by its affection it is conformed to what it loves. For it cannot love a good person because he is good, without being itself made good by that same goodness. Is not this the meaning of: "Think of the Lord in goodness,"[33] and "For to know you (i.e. Wisdom) is perception perfected,"[34] and also of the words of the Apostle: "Let this mind be in you, which was also in Christ Jesus."?[35] This is the charity by which he who loves "abides in God and God in him."[36]

9. O Charity, Charity, you have brought us to this that, because we love God and the Son of God, we are called and we are gods and the sons of God![37] Although "it does not yet appear what we shall be, when he shall appear we shall be like him, for we shall see him as he is."[38] Lord, it is good for us to be here![39] We wish we could stay here, we wish that we might die![40] But I beseech you, Lord, to grant to those who think and speak and write of you a balanced judgment, an utterance concise and disciplined, and a heart aflame

---

31. The expression "sense of the soul"—*sensus animae*—might surprise us. The reality for William of St Thierry as for St Augustine is that all the sensible knowledge of which the body is the cause is transmitted to the soul. See Augustine's *De Genesi ad Litt. Lib. Impef.*, 5, 24 (PL 34:228).

32. 2 Cor 3:18.	33. Wis 1:1.
34. Wis 6:16.	35. Phil 2:5.
36. 1 Jn 4:16.	37. Ps 81:6; 1 Jn 3:1.
38. 1 Jn 3:2.	39. Mt 17:4; Mk 9:4; Lk 9:33.

40. There is a play on words in the latin here which is totally lost in the translation: "*Libet hic immorari, et utinam liceret immori.*

to find you, Jesus, in the Scriptures that speak concerning you.[41]
Forgive, O Lord, forgive. The love of your love drives me; you
know, you see how things are with me. I am no scrutinizer of your
majesty;[42] a pauper is what I am, seeking your grace. I beg you by
the sweetness of your sweetest tenderness, do not let me be crushed
by your majesty, rather let me be supported by your grace. Forgive
me, I say, for to see God—here in a riddle only but hereafter face to
face[43]—is faith's proper desire. Do not flatter yourself, O man, do
not be over-confident. Do not imagine you can stay here, however
much you may be a man of desire like Daniel;[44] do not ever say:
"It is enough!" Whatever awareness you have here of seeing God,
whatever faith here teaches you about him, is a riddle, darker at
times indeed, at others clearer. They only know who have experienced it, how sweet that vision is when it is present, and how much
it is to be desired when it seems to be withdrawn. For this experience
is the stone with the name written upon it, which no man knows
save he who has received it.[45]

10. And it is said of the vision that shall be face to face: "No man
shall see me, and live."[46] For he who sees will not live, but will say:
"O wretched man that I am! Who will deliver me from the body
of this death?",[47] hoping exceedingly that, when at last he sees God
perfectly, then he will live indeed. How does perception come in to
all this? Of what avail are mental images? Can reason, or rational
understanding,[48] effect anything? No. For although reason sends us
to you, O God, it cannot of itself attain to you. Neither does that
understanding which, as a product of reason, has lower matters for
its sphere of exercise, go any further than does reason itself; it is
powerless to attain to you. But the understanding which is from

41. Lk 24:27, 32. William here formulates a brief but very beautiful prayer
which every preacher and theological writer could well make his own.

42. Prov 25:27.

43. 1 Cor 12:13.

44. Dan 9:23; 10:11, 19.

45. Rev 2:17.

46. Ex 33:20.

47. Rom 7:24.

48. "Rational understanding" as opposed to the understanding which comes
from God of which William will speak shortly. See also *Meditation 2:8*,
above, p. 100.

H

above[49] carries the fragrance of its place of origin; there is nothing human in its operation, it is all divine. And, where it is inpoured, it carries along with itself its own reasons which function independently of the inferior reason, except insofar as the obedience of faith requires.

11. This sort of understanding makes neither division nor conjunction in the Trinity. But, when and how and as far as the Holy Spirit wills, it controls the believing mind, so that something of what you are may be seen by those who in their prayer and contemplation have got past all that you are not, although they do not see you as you are. Nevertheless this understanding serves to soothe the loving spirit, for there is clearly nothing in it of that which you are not and, although it is not wholly what you are, it is not different from that Reality.[50]

12. For the Spirit of the Lord of a sudden so clothes[51] the tranquil, humble man on whom he rests,[52] and so changes him into another man,[53] that no antithesis is felt in the believer's mind. The Trinity in no way contradicts the Unity, nor does it put a stumbling-block before the piety of him who seeks the one God. The unity of substance does not dim the charity of him who rejoices in the love between the Father and the Son. Neither the onlyness nor the plurality disturbs him, but the oneness of the Trinity and the three-foldness of the Unity so avail for him, that with a loving and sober

49. Jas 3:17.

50. The soul which advances in love becomes more and more able to sense and experience the things of God. William is speaking here of an interior perceptivity which is always united to love. See on this matter St Augustine's *Enarratio in Ps.* 99 (PL 37:1274).

51. Judg 6:34: "The Spirit of the Lord clothed Gideon"; 2 Chron 24:20: "The Spirit of God clothed Zechariah." That "a sudden"—*repente*—applied to the Holy Spirit is inspired by the experience of Pentecost: "And suddenly there came a sound from heaven."—*Et factus est repente de coelo sonitus . . .* (Acts 2:2).

52. Is 66:2. This is a favorite with the Cistercian Fathers and they frequently comment on it. See for example St Bernard: *Homilies on the Annunciation* 1:5; *Sermon on the Nativity of the Blessed Virgin Mary* 4:9; 6:10; *Sermon for Pentecost* 3:1; Aelred of Rievaulx: *Sermons on Isaiah*, Ser. 14 (Cistercian Fathers Series 26).

53. 1 Sam 10:6.

understanding he comprehends the majesty of the divine incomprehensibility by the very fact that he does not comprehend it. And as he thus tastes and sees how gracious the Lord is,[54] all of a sudden his whole being grows so sweet in tasting of his sweetness, and he is so lit up by seeing the light of his truth, and so beside himself in the joy of the Holy Spirit at this sudden plenitude of the highest Good, that he is confident he will have won eternal life, if this experience be perfected. For "this is life eternal, that they may know you the only true God, and Jesus Christ whom you have sent."[55] "Come to him," therefore, "and be enlightened, and your faces shall not be ashamed."[56]

---

54. Ps 33:9.　　　55. Jn 17:3.　　　56. Ps 33:6.

MEDITATION FOUR

*William asks for the gift of prayer, and describes his
former state of recent desolation.*

LORD, YOU ARE PITYING and merciful, patient and
kind beyond all measure. You are gracious to all, and your
compassions rest on all your works.[1] You yourself exhort
us, Lord, to pray and to watch in prayer; so does your Holy Spirit.[2]
You exhort us and teach us to do so, out of your tenderness and
pity and your will to show us mercy. And you make out our case
beforehand for us, establishing for us judgment and justice,[3] so that,
if we pray as we should, you may have just cause for showing mercy.
And you have fixed for us even our form of prayer,[4] so that you,
who are for us both judge and advocate, may in no respect fail us
in our cause. And you have told us to ask boldly in your name, and
to believe that we shall receive whatever we have asked, and that
those things for which we pray will come to pass.[5]

2. It is your goodness, Lord, that leads you to do this; we, on the
other hand, are bound by grim necessity. And yet, in spite of all
your exhortation, we are slow to pray; in spite of your bidding
we neglect to do it, and we do not believe your promises. Nevertheless, you in your mercy and your great compassion rouse the
slothful and the negligent; your patience overlooks our lack of
trust.[6] And further, since we neither know how to pray aright, nor

1. Ps 144:8f.

2. Mt 26:41; Mk 14:38; Lk 21:36; Eph 6:18; Col 4:2; 1 Pet 4:7.

3. Ps 118:121. 4. Mt 6:9; Lk 11:2.

5. Jn 14:13, 16:23; Mk 11:24. 6. Wis 11:24.

have the power to do so, you send your Holy Spirit, that he may help our weakness and intercede for us with groanings that cannot be uttered.[7]

We pray, therefore, because you tell us to do so; we ask with confidence, because we have your promise; and forthwith you run to meet us and answer our prayer, finding in us a ground for your forgiveness, because you have yourself made us forgivable.

3. Loving as you are, O Lord, now you multiply your loving-kindness on us all, and we begin to see your mercies that are over all your works.[8] For when, O God, instead of fleeing from us, you begin to draw near and to rejoice our spirits with your consolation,[9] the soul's dead senses catch the fragrance of your healing presence and perceive its touch, and forthwith come to life; faith leaps up and confidence is cheered; the heart is kindled, and tears run down to fan the new-lit fire, not to quench it.

When your Spirit helps our weakness thus, your sweetness moves us to weep copious floods of sweet and fruitful tears; and when your loving-comfort wipes the tears away, they flow the more profusely and become our meat by day and night,[10] a strong and pleasant food. For it is a happy thing for us who are your people and the sheep of your pasture, O Lord our God, to weep before you who are our Creator.[11]

4. I, even I, O Lord, am, as your Prophet[12] has said, a man that sees my own poverty; I am poor and beset with troubles from my youth; having been lifted up, I have been humbled and put to shame.[13] For you have brought me through such great and dire

---

7. Gal 4:6; Rom 8:26.   8. Ps 144:9.   9. Ps 93:19.

10. Ps 41:4.   11. Ps 94:7 (Gallican Psalter).   12. Jeremiah: Lam 3:1.

13. Ps 87:16. Here begins an autobiographical section. William at first makes allusion to his abbacy at St Thierry. The many concerns of those years he felt worked to the detriment of his spiritual life. Entering at Signy, he "found his life again." Before becoming abbot of St Thierry he had been a monk at St Nicasius. It is that to which he refers when he speaks of having first been created by God in a paradise. Later when he became abbot of St Thierry, he tasted "the fruit of the tree of the knowledge of good and evil" (See his treatise, *On the Nature and Dignity of Love*, n. 25 (Cistercian Fathers Series 15): "to taste of this fruit is proper to superiors."). Finally he entered upon the Cistercian way of life at Signy: "I hid myself among the trees of paradise."

troubles, and then you have turned and led me back to life, you have brought me again from the deep of the earth. You have multiplied your mighty acts upon me; turning toward me, you have brought me comfort.[14] For when of old in your paradise you created me, and gave me the tree of life for my possession, as of abiding right, you willed—or at least you allowed me—to reach my hand out also for the fruit of the tree of the knowledge of good and evil; you did this, so that I, who had grown weary of my inward blessings, might find what sort of outward action I could do, with the consent and help of Eve, my flesh.[15] I tasted of the fruit and saw, not your graciousness but my own shame.[16] I saw myself as one whose infamy needed a cloak to cover it, whose nakedness trembled to meet you, whose liberty required the constraint of laws. For I was found in your sight destitute of all the inward things men thought that I possessed; I was found shameful in my inward parts and found in them no refuge from myself, nor yet from you. And I, who had received the charge of ruling others, appeared as needing to be ruled myself!

5. Therefore, O Lord, I hid myself among the trees of paradise, therefore I fled away to my dark places, I "got me away far off," not from you, Lord, but to you, and abode in the wilderness. And there I wait for you, who have saved me from faintheartedness and from the storm.[17] I have put my mouth in the dust, if so there may be hope,[18] a lone wild ass, snuffing the breeze of my love.[19] And when I come wholly to myself again, I sit alone and do not speak.[20] I hear neither the cry of the driver [21] nor the din of battle. I see that the time serves me when I thus have leisure to attend to myself and I ask: "Who am I?" and "Whence have I come?" I recognize myself as one of the sons of Adam, a child of wrath by nature,[22] but a servant of your holy Church by grace. I know myself to be one of

---

14. Ps 70:20f.   15. Cf. Gen 2:17; 3:1ff.

16. The allusion is still to Genesis where Adam ate and also Eve and they saw their nudity; but the expression is taken from Ps 33:9: "Taste and see how sweet is the Lord."

17. Ps 54:8f.   18. Lam 3:29.   19. Jer 2:24.

20. Lam 3:28.   21. Job 39:7.   22. Eph 2:3.

those exiled from paradise, living and toiling on the earth which is accursed, for you have laid a curse on it in all the works of Adam.[23] When I have tilled it, it does not yield its fruits, but brings forth thorns and thistles for me in their stead. In the sweat of my brow I eat my bread,[24] according to the stern decree of your just judgment by which you have rebuked the proud and the accursed who do not keep your commandments.[25]

6. O good Creator! How well had you created me! How gloriously had you fashioned me![26] How blessed a place had you appointed for my dwelling! You created me, Lord, for the good works you had prepared for me to walk in, as the Apostle says.[27] You fashioned me in your own image and likeness,[28] and set me in the paradise of your delight, that I might till it and guard it, till it with my good endeavors, and guard it,[29] lest the serpent should steal in. The serpent did steal in, seduced my Eve, and made me a sinner through her.[30] For that reason I am driven out of the paradise of good conscience, and made to be an exile in a foreign country,[31] the land of unlikeness.[32]

7. But, Lord, you who made all things and saw all your works, that they were very good,[33] will you let my ill-doing ruin your

---

23. Gen 3:17.   24. Gen 3:18f.   25. Ps 118:21.

26. In this lively passage which borders on the dramatic William transposes and applies the elevation and fall of Adam to himself. Without the sin of Adam, which has become for him the original sin, *peccatum originatum*, he would have been created in "beauty," in justice. The fall of the first man, original sin, *peccatum originans*, established in him, William, an unbalance of powers, an unbalance which he began to experience at the dawn of the use of reason. He asks to recover that harmony which belongs to the state of original justice.

27. Eph 2:10.   28. Gen 1:26.   29. Gen 2:15.
30. Gal 2:18.   31. Ps 136:4.

32. "The land of unlikeness" is a theme which reoccurs not only in the works of William but in those of many of the Cistercian Fathers. The soul ravaged by original sin retains its three faculties by which it remains made in the image of God. But these instead of being directed toward him turn themselves toward creatures as their last end. This is exile in "the land of unlikeness." See *The Nature of Body and Soul*, n. 16 (Cistercian Fathers Series 24); *Exposition on the Song of Songs*, n. 65 (Cistercian Fathers Series 6), p. 52 and the note there.   33. Gen 1:31.

good work? Truly, you did not make me for paradise, but paradise for me, when you made me man, to be supreme on earth! O Lord, do not repent of having made me so,[34] but bid me to be a reasonable man, as at the first, ruling my earth[35] so that I may subject my body to my spirit and my spirit to you. Do not regret the dignity you have bestowed on man in giving me dominion over the beasts of my earth, that is to say, the fierce and untamed movements of my soul's affections. Do not repent of having given me dominion also over those reptiles, the thoughts that creep along the ground and are noxious and deadly with the poison of the earth to which they cleave; dominion, moreover, over the fishes of the sea and the birds of heaven, worldly thoughts that explore and pursue the secrets of the world and the pride of its day, and over the beasts of burden, namely those powers of the body which you created in us that they might bear our burdens, as their name implies.[36] O you who gave us all these faculties, make them submit to the bridle of reason, the goads of holy zeal, and the stall of discipline, and in that stall let them feed on their proper foods and be nourished by them, so that they may be led thence to work when occasion requires, but never allowed to roam at large in the broad ways of error![37] The day will come, says he who gives the promise, the day will come when the lion and lamb will lie down together,[38] when hurtful things will hurt no one at all in all your holy mountain.[39] Even the beasts of burden will browse in luscious pastures[40] then, being instruments no longer of our weakness,[41] but rather of our blessed happiness.

---

34. Gen 6:6.

35. An allusion to Gen 1:26: "We have made man . . . have placed him over the fishes of the sea, etc."; the expressions are taken rather from Gen 34:10.

36. *Jumentum*, the Latin word for a beast of burden, is considered here to come from *juvare*.

37. William, as all the Fathers of the Cistercian School, was not marked with any Manichean disdain for the body but rather maintained a healthy hierarchy between body and soul in their service. See above, *On Contemplating God*, p. 36; and also the *Exposition on the Song of Songs*, n. 54 (Cistercian Fathers Series 6), p. 44 and the note there.

38. Is 11:6.   39. Is 11:9.   40. Ezek 34:14.

41. That is to say reinforce or accentuate our weakness.

8. Meanwhile, Lord, "hear the heavens, and let the heavens hear the earth. Let the earth hear the wine and the corn, and let these hear Jezreel,"[42] that is, the seed of God that you have sown in us. For, as the Prophet says, you, Lord, allured me, and brought me into the wilderness, promising to speak there to your servant's heart.[43] And now I thank you that you have so spoken, once and again, and indeed many times; and, when my soul tells you: "You are my God,"[44] you sometimes answer with a gentle kindness: "I am your salvation."[45]

9. And now, Desire of my soul,[46] my soul desires to wait on you a little space, and to taste and see how gracious you are, O Lord.[47] She implores your tender mercy to give me peace and silence from all things, whether outward or inward. She begs you to keep for me that power over the things within me that you have given me, but outwardly to make a covenant between me and every beast of the field, every creeping thing of earth, and every bird of heaven, and to banish the bow and the sword and war from my earth,[48] that my whole place may be in peace and my dwelling in Sion.[49] Give me, O Lord, the comfort of my wilderness—a solitary heart and frequent communing with you. As long as you are with me, O my God, I shall not be alone; but, if you leave me, woe to him that is alone; for, if I fall asleep, there will be none to keep me warm; if I fall down, there will be nobody to pick me up.[50]

---

42. Hos 2:21f. In the Vulgate text it is God who is speaking. "Under this figurative language the Prophet alludes to a state of perfect harmony which is meant to reign between the moral and physical world. William takes up the allegory and applies it to the human composite. A day will come when for the Christian who is striving towards perfection that harmony between the lower powers of man and the higher faculties will flourish again according to the order which prevailed in the state of original justice."—Déchanet, *Meditations et Prières*, p. 130.

43. Hos 2:14. William speaks here of his retreat to Signy. Cf. this with *Meditation Thirteen* below, p. 186. There it is a question rather of a storm and a trial that he finds rather than this serenity of which he speaks here.

44. Ps 15:2; Hos 2:24.   45. Ps 34:3.   46. Is 26:9.

47. Ps 33:9.   48. Hos 2:18.   49. Ps 75:3.

50. Eccles 4:10f. See above, *Meditation Two*, 2, p. 95 and the note there.

10. Lead me away, meanwhile, my refuge and my strength,[51] into the heart of the desert as once you led your servant Moses; lead me where the bush burns, yet is not burnt up,[52] where the holy soul that has earned admission to a like experience is all aflame with the fullness of the fire of your Holy Spirit, and, burning like the seraphim,[53] is not consumed but cleansed. And then there comes to pass for the first time a better thing, the miracle of all your miracles, the sight of sights. The soul attains to the holy place where none may stand or take another step, except he be bare-footed[54]—having loosed the shoe-strings of all fleshly hindrances—the place, that is, that the soul may enter only with her affections clean and pure.[55] This is the place where He Who Is, who cannot be seen as he is, is notwithstanding heard to say, "I Am Who Am,"[56] the place where, for the time, the soul must cover her face so that she does not see the face of God,[57] and yet in humble obedience must use her ears to hear what the Lord God will say concerning her.[58]

11. Hide me then in the day of evil, O Lord, in the secret place of your tabernacle, in the hidden recesses of your face far from the strife of tongues;[59] for your yoke is easy and the burden you have laid on me is light.[60] And when you show me the difference between your service and the service of the world,[61] gently and tenderly you ask me if it is not better to serve you, the living God, than to serve strange gods.[62]

And I, for my part, adore the hand that lays the load, I kiss the yoke, and I embrace the burden; and it is very sweet to me to sweat beneath its weight. For masters other than you have long possessed

---

51. Ps 45:2.   52. Ex 3:1f.

53. Seraphim comes from *serafin*, which signifies to burn. See above, *On Contemplating God,* 6, p. 44.

54. Ex 3:5.

55. Here is simply defined the ascetical preparation that must precede the mystical life.

56. Ex 3:14.   57. Ex 3:6.   58. Ps 84:9.

59. Ps 30:21.   60. Mt 11:30.   61. 2 Chron 12:8.

62. "To serve strange gods" is an expression which is frequent in Scripture especially in Deut 7:4; 13:6; 17:3, etc.

me,[63] and their yoke is not easy, nor is their burden light. I desire to be subject to your law; I acknowledge your yoke, and your light burden that lifts me up and does not crush me down.

12. And when first I put myself to school in your service, I seem to see a new earth and new heavens, for of a sudden you make all things new for me.[64] I am a countryman, Lord, who comes from the country of the world. Teach me your city's ordered ways, the courtesies and gracious manners of your court. Remove from me the likeness of the world, on which I had been modelling myself, and make me like your citizens, lest in their midst I seem as one deformed. And teach me too the language that I do not know, the language I began to hear when I came out of Egypt,[65] but do not understand because I had grown up in an alien land.[66] Teach me the language you speak with your sons, and they with you, and make me understand those little signs, by which you give understanding hearts to know what is your good, acceptable and perfect will.[67]

13. And now, O tender Father, thanks to you my soul begins to hear your voice when you address her, but she does not fully understand what you are saying to her. For your voice never comes empty;[68] your voice is your grace, and it is heard, not outwardly, but sweetly and effectively within. Moreover, when I speak to you, I turn towards you, and that too is good for me. And whatever the object of my prayer, I never pray or worship you in vain; the very act of praying brings me rich reward.[69] Teach me then, Holy Spirit, to pray without ceasing,[70] that you may grant me to rejoice unceasingly in you.[71] For though your poor man, being poor in spirit,[72] makes lamentation when he prays, either because he remembers his sins, or else because he finds himself in straits, nevertheless his joy is keener in proportion to his grief. But on the other hand the man who rejoices in the world is—if he has any sense at all—the more tormented and grieved in the depths of his conscience in proportion to his joy. Devout and single-minded prayer is never without joy.

63. Is 26:13.   64. Rev 21:1, 5.   65. Ps 80:6.
66. Bar 3:11.   67. Rom 12:2.   68. Is 55:11.
69. Ps 18:12.   70. 1 Thess 5:17.   71. 1 Thess 5:16.   72. Mt 5:3.

MEDITATION FIVE

The different kinds of prayer.
Christ's passion and William's sins.

WHEN I DESIRE to stir my heart to constant and effective prayer, to practice it and establish the habit, I would have no direction except yours, Lord Jesus, the Wisdom of God the Father.[1] I call to mind, therefore, the kinds of prayer you practiced among men on earth, and by which you gave us a pattern for perfect prayer. I find you praying sometimes alone[2] and sometimes in a crowd,[3] sometimes in exaltation of spirit,[4] at one time in a sweat of blood,[5] and at another lifted up upon the cross.[6]

2. Exaltation of spirit and praying alone are very pleasant indeed for me to imitate; but, unless you prevent me with the blessings of your sweetness,[7] though I shall find a solitary place with ease, I shall not find a solitary heart. Exaltation of spirit proceeds either from purity of conscience, which I do not find in myself, or else from the abundance of your grace, of which I am unworthy.

3. You, to whom no grace was lacking, were able to pray in a crowd; we ourselves do not avoid such prayer, if the occasion demands it. I know, O Lord, I know that your prayer in the bloody sweat and your prayer on the cross are utterly needful for me; for, when I think what there is in me that needs to be sweated out in

1. 2 Cor 1:24.   2. Mt 14:23.   3. Jn 11:41f.; 12:27ff.
4. Lk 10:21.   5. Lk 22:42ff.   6. Lk 23:34, 46.
7. Ps 20:4.

prayer and forced out by the anguish of the cross, my heart sweats tears of blood before your look, although I do not have a bloody sweat.

So too with crucifixion; it is not my body that is crucified, but my wretched soul that is put to greater inward agony than that of any cross. Yet I am crucified with you,[8] Lord Jesus, at least upon the cross of my profession. By your gift of grace daily and constantly I offer it to you. These are your gifts, your presents. But when from my own pleasant cross I look at the cross of your passion, the nails of fear of you pierce me.[9] I am confounded and all my spirit quails, not from the pain of my cross (which by your grace is nothing to me now[10]) but because of the pain of my heart. I consider your work revived in the midst of the years,[11] revealed in redemption's effect throughout all time, both before as well as after the event, your work that no one can repay and to which no death, no life can ever make adequate response, your work which, nonetheless, is despised by the very world it has redeemed.

4. The force of habit has inured us to the sight of you upon the cross, to the thought of you as dead and buried and—what should pierce our hearts even more readily and deeply—to the thought of you who on the cross thirsted for nothing but our salvation,[12] as buffeted and scourged, as mocked and spit upon, pierced by the nails and spear, crowned with the thorns, and given gall or vinegar to drink. The earth trembled when you were crucified;[13] we laugh. The heavens and its lights were darkened;[14] we want to shine before the world. The rocks were rent;[15] but we harden our hearts. The

---

8. Gal 2:19.   9. Ps 118:120; Gal 2:19.

10. An allusion to the trial which the former Abbot of St Thierry experienced a short time after his entrance at Signy. William was at the point of being completely discouraged and despairing when a vision comforted him. The grace of the vision was so abundant that afterwards he was able to bear with ease the heavy yoke of Cistercian discipline.

11. Hab 3:2.

12. Jn 19:28. William interprets the *sitio* of Christ as a thirst for souls.

13. Mt 27:51. The expression William uses, *terra tremuit*, is drawn from Ps 75:9.

14. Lk 23:45; Mt 27:45; Mk 15:33.   15. Mt 27:51.

opened graves gave up their dead;[16] but we, taking our ease on the bed of self-indulgence,[17] bury our dead.[18]

5. You offered three prayers to God the Father during your passion, Lord, if I remember right; and all agree that those three prayers include all that your passion should effect, at the price of your blood, for yourself,[19] for your friends,[20] and for your enemies.[21] When you prayed for yourself, you did not have to labor, for, as the Apostle says, you were heard by reason of your godly fear.[22] You prayed also for your friends, who continued with you in your temptations,[23] and for the enemies who crucified you, but knew not what they did.[24] When did you pray for those who sin knowingly? Such persons, as long as they continue in their sin, are outside the embrace of the crucified who, with his hands outstretched upon the cross, seemed by the very shape of the gibbet to embrace all for whom he was enduring it.

Therefore the Apostle says: "No sacrifice for sin remains for those who sin deliberately."[25] Unless repentance washes their sins away, unless a sweat of blood expels and the pain of the cross forces out the evil from their systems, I cannot see that those who sin deliberately and knowingly have any share either in the prayer of him who sweat his blood, or in the sacrifice of him who hung upon the cross.

6. Alas for me! My conscience accuses me, and Truth does not excuse me so that he can say: "For he knew not what he did." By virtue of the price of your precious blood, therefore, forgive me all my sins, O Lord, whether committed knowingly or not. Tell your sinner, whisper in your servant's ear what he must do to make amends for them, above all for those that he committed, knowing what he did. For if, as it appears, you have excluded conscious sinners from your mercy, woe to the whole wide world, for it

16. Mt 27:52.   17. Amos 6:4.

18. "Bury our dead" seems to be an allusion to Mt 8:22: "Let the dead bury their dead."

19. Mk 14:36.   20. Jn 17:9.   21. Lk 23:34.

22. Heb 5:7.   23. Lk 22:28.   24. Lk 23:34.

25. Heb 10:26.

would seem you have included very few! "No sacrifice avails for those who sin deliberately," the Apostle says. "A man who makes void the Law of Moses dies without any mercy at the deposition of two or three witnesses. How much more, do you think, is he deserving of worse punishments who has trodden underfoot, the Son of God, and has treated as worthless the blood of the covenant by which he was sanctified, and has offered an affront to the Spirit of grace? For we know who said: 'Vengeance is mine; I will repay!' "[26]

7. Lord, truly I have sinned by my own will and much, after I had received the knowledge of the truth, and I have offered an affront to the Spirit of grace. After receiving from him the free remission of my sins in baptism, after receiving the knowledge of the truth, I have returned to those sins like a dog to his vomit.[27] But have I spurned you also, Son of God? I have spurned you, if I have denied you, although I should not think that Peter trod you underfoot, for all that he came to deny you. He loved you most ardently even while declaring once, twice, and even thrice that he did not know you.[28] Have I "treated as worthless the blood of the covenant"?[29] May he who thinks thus, be anathema! God forbid that such a thought should ever be in my heart, or that my lips should ever make such an admission!

Satan has sought out my faith sometimes, to sift it as wheat; but your prayer has reached even to me, so that my faith in you should never fail.[30] Virtue consists in the willing assent of the mind to what is good.[31] You know that my mind has always wanted to abide in your faith; preserve it in me unto the end. I have always believed in you, I have never denied you; I have always loved you, even when I sinned against you. I shall be sorry for my sin until I die; but I shall never repent of having loved you, unless it be because even in death I did not love you as I ought. If I had so loved you, I should not have sinned. And yet, alas, I am afraid my very love of you will bring

---

26. Heb 10:26ff.   27. Prov 26:11; 2 Pet 2:22.
28. Mk 14:66ff.   29. Heb 10:29.
30. Lk 22:31f.   31. The classical Augustinian definition of virtue.

me into judgment; for, if it be so serious a thing to sin after receiving knowledge of the truth, how much more serious is it so to do after one has tasted of your goodness and received the sweetness of your love![32]

8. For even in my childhood your grace enabled me to love you, unclean child though I was; and yet my sins against you were not childish sins. From that time till this present I have never ceased to sin,[33] and you have never ceased to work my good. What then is left for me, except to hear: "You in your lifetime received your good things"?[34]

But turn your judgment into mercy, Lord, and condemn sin by sin.[35] Although you have good reason to condemn me by reason of the smallness of my love for you may I now by your grace receive the fullness of your love, and so come to your judgment-seat and appear in your holy place [36] and before the eyes of your mercy with the same right as the sinful woman of whom you said: "Her many sins are forgiven, because she loved much."[37] But first, Lord, let the fire of your perfect love inflame my heart, let its great heat sweat and cook out of me all the poison of sin; let it search out and wash away with the tears of my eyes all that defiles my conscience. May your cross drive from me all the evil that I have contracted through the lust of the flesh, the lust of the eyes, and the pride of life,[38] through the long-continued rusting of my negligence. May whatever has been charred and sapped[39] by the will of the flesh[40]

---

32. Heb 6:4f.: "For it is impossible for those who were once enlightened, who have both tasted the heavenly gift and become partakers of the Holy Spirit, who have moreover tasted the good word of God...." William contrasts the sin committed after one has received knowledge of the truth (Heb 10:26: "after having received knowledge of the truth") to that committed, still voluntarily, after one has experienced the divine intimacy and the sweetness of God (Heb 6:4f.).

33. This statement is not to be accepted literally of course just as one would not think of taking St Bernard literally when he wrote: "I ask that you pray for me without ceasing for I have not ceased to sin."—Letter 27.

34. Lk 16:25.   35. Rom 8:3.   36. Ps 62:3.

37. Lk 7:47.   38. 1 Jn 2:16.   39. Ps 79:17.

40. Jn 1:13.

and the mind's consent thereto perish at the rebuke of your countenance!

9. Lord, anyone who likes may hear me thus confessing, and may laugh at me! Anyone may see me lying with the sinful woman at your mercy's feet, washing them with the tears of my heart and anointing them with the perfume of heartfelt devotion! Let me give my whole substance (whatever that amounts to!) alike in body and soul, to buy the perfume that you will accept, that I may pour it out upon your head, whose head is God,[41] and on your feet, whose lower part is our humble nature.

Let the Pharisee murmur,[42] but do you have mercy on me, O my God![43] Let the thief with his money-bag gnash his teeth at me if he likes;[44] as long as you are pleased with me, I care very little who may be displeased. O my heart's love, may I anoint you daily, ceaselessly, for, when I am anointing you, I anoint myself. My nature, hardened by long wickedness, is like a leather bottle in the winter;[45] unless the sweet and constant influence of this ointment softens it, it freezes and grows hard, it cracks, spilling whatever of your goodness it might seem to have contained.

10. You said: "She has done what she could."[46] Grant, Lord, that I may faithfully devote to you all that I have, all that I know, all that I am, and all that I can do; let me keep nothing for myself. I stand to be judged by you, and by no man; I lie at your mercy's feet, and there I will lie and lament, until you make me hear your blessed voice, the judgment of your lips, the declaration of your righteous-

---

41. 1 Cor 11:3. William does not take the text here exactly as it is found in 1 Cor where it is a question of God being the head of Christ, but rather he understands here Christ as having for his head (that which is the most elevated part of him) the divinity (the divine nature in Christ) and for his lower part our human nature. Cf. St Bernard, *Second Sermon for the Sunday after the Octave of the Epiphany*, 1: "How beautiful the feet . . . but much more beautiful and precious is his head, because the head of Christ is God."—*The Works of Bernard of Clairvaux*, vol. 4 (Cistercian Fathers Series 10).

42. Lk 7:39.

43. In many of the psalms one finds a cry for mercy expressed in this way: Ps 50:3; 55:2; 56:2.

44. Mk 14:5; Jn 12:4ff.   45. Ps 118:83.   46. Mk 14:8.

I

ness which is mine too, for you have given it to me: "Her many sins are forgiven, for she loved much."[47]

Lord, by all the judgment that the Father has committed to you,[48] give me this merit beforehand and judge me with this judgment; for out of love for your love I would rather be justified and saved by this criterion of love, than magnified and glorified by any other way. Do not shut me out, O Lord, from the embrace of your redemption, for I desire in everything to share your cross.

You said: "Vengeance is mine; I will repay."[49] No, no, most merciful! Mine be the vengeance that I may repent. "It is a fearful thing to fall into the hands of the living God."[50] Command me as you will; but give me sense to understand your bidding and power to perform it, even as you have already given me a heart prepared thereto,[51] so that neither my heart nor my body may draw back from doing your will in any particular. "You know my sitting down and my rising up, and all my thoughts both recent and long past."[52] Unmake me from the pattern of the world, on which I have modelled myself; make me and conform me to the pattern of your grace, to which I have now fled, and teach my heart the kind of penitence that pleases you. Give me also, Lord, a faith devout and pure, holy and strong and unassailable; so that, bestowing grace for grace,[53] you may say even to me: "Go, for your faith has made you whole."[54]

---

47. Lk 7:47.   48. Jn 5:27.

49. Rom 12:19; Deut 32:35; Heb 10:30.   50. Heb 10:31.

51. Cf. above *On Contemplating God*, 2, p. 37. The expression is of Augustinian inspiration: *De Natura et Gratia*, 43, 50.

52. Ps 138:3, 5.   53. Jn 1:16.   54. Lk 7:50.

MEDITATION SIX

The joy of the blessed.

"I SAW A DOOR OPENED in heaven," says blessed John, "and the first voice which I heard was as it were of a trumpet speaking to me, which said: 'Come up hither.' "[1] O Lord, you created the heavens and the earth,[2] yet you cursed the earth in Adam's sin and work.[3] You have appointed for his children's dwelling-place this earth whose inhabitants are all of them under a curse;[4] for they not only bear the ceaseless punishments of the ancient malediction, but also, by forsaking your commandments, incur fresh penalties from day to day, even as it is written: "Cursed are they who depart from your commandments."[5] I am weighed down with this plethora of curses new and old; the things that I never took I am compelled to pay,[6] my proper debts I must discharge with compound interest! How eagerly, how gladly would I escape from our earth to your heaven, the heaven that you have kept for yourself since the casting thence of the proud one purged it once for all from pride! If only I could find the way of ascent, and the open door!

2. They tell me there is nothing there of all the evils that we suffer here; there is no morning, nor yet evening there, no morning joy that passes, no evening griefs that last.[7] You know how I should rejoice to see the end of those and, in their place, a single day,[8] glad

1. Rev. 4:1.   2. Gen 1:1.   3. Gen 3:17.
4. Gen 3:10.   5. Ps 118:21.   6. Ps 68:5.
7. Ps 29:6.   8. Zech 14:7.

with the ceaseless glory of the sight of you, voided of all that could distract from feasting for ever on your face. No fire, no hail, no snow, no ice, no stormy winds ascend up there, they say, such as down here descend on us so constantly to trouble us at your behest.[9] There is no death nor corruption there, of either body or soul; all pestilent disorders are banished utterly; virtue alone is found, and happiness, and joy, and your own charity rejoicing in its proper good, unvexed by any fear of losing it.

3. I know, moreover, that that festal day is splendid with the angels' joyful praises, and glorious with the crowns of martyrs and apostles and of all good men who have found favor in your sight since time began. I know the Church is gathered there in one, and that she has established for that festal day her everlasting dwellings. Whenever we see two or three of that company gathered together in your name on earth, with you, Lord, in their midst,[10] their life together seems so good, so pleasant, so fragrant with the unction of the Holy Spirit, that it is plain to all that there the blessing that you have ordained is realized.[11] How much more, then, shall this be so, where you have gathered your saints, who have made a covenant with you by sacrifices, and where the heavens you have made proclaim your righteousness![12]

4. For that Beloved Disciple of yours[13] was not the only one to find the way to heaven, nor was the open door revealed to him alone. Not by a herald, nor by any prophet, but out of your own mouth to all and openly you have proclaimed: "I am the door; if anyone enters in by me, he shall be saved."[14] You are the door, then, Lord; and when you say: "if anyone enters in by me," you open, apparently, to all who will. But of what use is it to us who are on earth to see the door in heaven standing open, when we cannot get up there? Paul answers thus: "He who ascends is the same also as he who descended."[15] Who is he? He is love. For love in us mounts

---

9. Ps 148:8.   10. Mt 18:20.   11. Ps 132:1ff.

12. Ps 49:5f.   13. St John. See Rev 4:1.   14. Jn 10:9.

15. Eph 4:10. St Paul's formula: "He who descends, it is he also who ascends," is inverted by William.

up to you, O Lord, because the love in you comes down to us. You, who loved us, you came down to us; by loving you we shall mount up to you. You who yourself declared: "I am the door," by your own self I pray you, open yourself to us,[16] that you may show more clearly what house you open, and when you open, and to whom. The house of which you are the door is heaven, as we said before; and heaven is where the Father dwells, of whom we read: "The Lord's seat is in heaven."[17] And truly nobody comes to the Father except by you, who are the door.[18]

But one of your servants says that those who still take pleasure in the beauty of things seen cannot perceive God spiritually.[19] They prefer the earth to heaven. Their point of view would be more endurable, however, if they were to believe that the God, of whom they still form only a material image, was in heaven, rather than on earth.

5. For you, O Maker of all times and places, are neither moved by time nor limited by place. You are not held up in a material heaven, lest you should fall down, nor do you dwell in it in such a way as not yourself to fill both heaven and earth.[20] For you are present everywhere. If one may use that word at all of you, who are above all place. And everywhere you are in your entirety, if one may predicate entirety in or concerning you, who know no division into parts. Yet you yourself have taught us to say: "Our Father, who art in heaven,"[21] and this belief that God inhabits heaven is so general that all men hold it, even Jews and heathen. But different is the belief of those who propose falsehoods from that of those who profess the truth by these same words. Thus those who understand, understand the truth; but those who can not grasp or understand things as they are are able by the words to form an opinion that is to some degree quite tolerable. Whence the prophet who speaks of "our God in heaven,"[22] adds shortly after "who dwells in Jerusalem."[23]

---

16. Mt 25:11.   17. Ps 10:4.   18. Jn 14:6.

19. Cf. 1 Cor 2:10. The "servant" whom William refers to here is identified as St Augustine by Dom Déchanet.

20. Jer 23:24.   21. Mt 6:9.   22. Ps 113:11.   23. Ps 124:1f.

6. Then answer us who seek and yearn for you, I beg: "Master, where do you dwell?"[24] You answer promptly, saying: "I am in the Father, and the Father is in me";[25] and, in another place: "On that day you shall know that I am in the Father, and you in me, and I in you."[26] And yet again: "I in them, and you in me, that they may be made perfect in oneness."[27]

The Father, then, is where you are, and you are where the Father is. Nor is that all; for we are where you are, and you are where we are.[28] Since, then, Lord Jesus, you are in the Father and the Father is in you, O most high and undivided Trinity, you are yourself the place of your abode, you are yourself your heaven. Just as your being has no fount outside yourself, so do you need no place in which to dwell, save of and in yourself.

7. When, therefore, you dwell in us, we are your heaven, most assuredly. Yet you are not yourself sustained by dwelling in us; no, it is your sustaining that makes us a dwelling for you. And you too are our heaven, to which we may ascend, and in which we may dwell. As I see it then our dwelling in you or yours in us is heaven for us. But for you the heaven of heavens is your eternity, where you are what you are in your own self. The Father is in the Son and the Son in the Father; and the bond that unites you, Father and Son, is the Holy Spirit, who comes not as it were from somewhere else to be the link between you, but who exists as such by virtue of his unity of being with you both.

It is in the Holy Spirit too, who creates and sets in order the unity that makes us one among ourselves and in you. He makes us, who were by nature sons of wrath,[29] to be Sons of God by grace, as the Apostle says: "Behold what manner of love the Father has bestowed on us, that we should be called, and be, the sons of God."[30]

24. Jn 1:38. William struggles with this same question in his *Prayer*, see above, p. 73.

25. Jn 14:10f.   26. Jn 14:20.   27. Jn 17:23.

28. The Latin is much stronger: *locus ergo tuus, Pater est, et tu Patris; et non solum, sed etiam nos locus tuus sumus, et tu noster.*—literally: "Therefore your place, it is the Father, and you are the place of the Father and not only that but also we are your place, and you ours."

29. Eph 2:3.   30. 1 Jn 3:1.

We are sons by a gift, indeed, who is the Holy Spirit. And a little further on we read: "Beloved, now are we the sons of God, and it does not yet appear what we shall be. But we know that, when he shall appear, we shall be like him, for we shall see him as he is."[31]

8. But whereas the birth of the Son from the Father belongs to the eternal divine nature, our birth as sons of God is an adoption of grace. The former birth is not something that happens, nor does it effect a unity; it is itself a oneness in the Holy Spirit. The latter birth, however, has no existence of itself, but comes to being through the Holy Spirit, in so far as it is stamped with the likeness of God. This unity of course transcends the limits of our human nature, but falls short of the unity that belongs to the being of God. The Holy Spirit is also called the seed of this birth, for the Apostle says of him: "Whosoever is born of God does not commit sin, for his seed remains in him, and therefore he cannot sin."[32] Moreover, the likeness of God will be conferred on us by the sight of God, when we not only see that he exists, but see him as he is; that is the likeness that will make us like to him. For for the Father to see the Son is to be what the Son is, and vice versa. For us, however, to see God is to be like God. This unity, this likeness is itself the heaven where God dwells in us, and we in him.

9. O Truth supreme, you are the heaven of heavens, you who are what you are, who have your being from yourself, who belong to yourself and are sufficient to yourself. You lack nothing, yet you have no excess; there is in you no discord nor confusion, no vacillation, no change nor shadow of turning, no need, no death; rather, you have within yourself supremest concord, utmost clarity, most perfect fullness and completest life. No foulness in your creation affects you; no malice hurts you, nor does any error make you go astray. For you have pre-ordained for all the righteous their own abodes of virtue or of blessing, and they must come to them, whatever circumstances let or hinder them. And for the wicked in their evil too you have appointed bounds which, even if they will, they cannot overpass.[33]

---

31. I Jn 3:2.   32. I Jn 3:9.   33. Job 14:5.

10. O Lord, this height, this depth, this wisdom and this might,[34] are these the heaven of which you are the door? It is so, truly; that is why the ark of the covenant was seen in heaven when the door was opened, as the same John says.[35] For what does the ark of the covenant that was seen in heaven mean, if not, as the Apostle says: "the dispensation of the mystery, which from the beginning has been hidden in God, who created all things";[36] You are yourself that ark. In you from all eternity was hidden, and in you in these latter days has been fulfilled, all that from the beginning of the world has been revealed to all the saints and prophets by the Law and by the prophecies,[37] by wonders and by signs. You are that ark in which every part is covered with pure gold;[38] for the fullness of God's Wisdom rested on you and invested you completely with its glory. In you is the vessel of gold that contains the manna, the holy and spotless soul in which the fullness of the Godhead dwelt corporeally.[39] In you is Aaron's rod that budded, the dignity of the eternal priesthood.[40] In you are the tables of the covenant, by which the world is made heir of your grace, and the nations are made coinheritors and fellow-heirs and sharers of your promise.[41] Above all these things are the bright cherubim, the plenitude of knowledge; but they are not above them because of their own excellence and worth, but rather as needing to be carried and upheld by them; their overshadowing of the mercy-seat testifies to the incomprehensibility of the mysteries of your atoning grace.

11. These blessings, that were hidden in your secret heaven through the ages, you at the ages' end unveiled to the world's longing eyes, when you opened in heaven the door that is yourself. You opened that door when your grace appeared to all men, teaching us;[42] when your kindness and love appeared, saving us not by works of righteousness that we have done, but according to

---

34. Cf. Rom 11:33.   35. Rev 11:19.

36. Eph 3:9.   37. Rom 3:21.

38. This whole passage is made up of texts taken from Heb 9:4f.

39. Col 2:9.   40. An allusion to Ps 109:4; see also Heb 5:6; 7:21.

41. Eph 3:6.   42. Tit 2:11f.

your mercy.[43] The heavens being thus opened, all the good and glory and delight of heaven poured itself out on earth. And then, O God, you who spared not your own Son, but delivered him up for us all,[44] the greatness of your kindness in respect to us was published openly to all. You made known your salvation to the world, and in the sight of all the nations you revealed your righteousness,[45] which you had made over to us by the blood of your sole-begotten Son. And he himself rendered to you for our salvation the pure obedience that proceeds from love,[46] and gave to us the love that sprang from his obedience. And then you blessed our earth;[47] thenceforward she began to yield her fruit.[48] Thenceforward the high road to heaven lay open to all men, the high road trodden by the feet of martyrs and apostles and all the saints who, by your example and the grace of charity received from you, have set themselves at nought for love of you, and have not been afraid to give their lives for you.[49]

Those unsearchable riches of your glory, Lord, were hidden in your secret place in heaven until the soldier's spear opened the side of your Son our Lord and Savior on the cross, and from it flowed the mysteries of our redemption.[50] Now we may not only thrust our finger or our hand into his side, like Thomas,[51] but through that open door may enter whole, O Jesus, even into your heart, the sure seat of your mercy, even into your holy soul that is filled with the fullness of God,[52] full of grace and truth,[53] full of our salvation and our consolation.

12. Open, O Lord, the ark-door of your side,[54] that all your own who shall be saved may enter in, before this flood that overwhelms the earth.[55] Open to us your body's side, that those who long to see the secrets of your Son may enter in, and may receive the sacraments that flow therefrom, even the price of their redemption.[56] Open the door of your heaven, that your redeemed may see the

---

43. Tit 3:4.

44. Rom 8:32.

45. Ps 97:2.

46. Cf. 1 Pet 1:22.

47. Ps 84:2.

48. Ps 84:13.

49. Jn 15:13.

50. Jn 19:34.

51. Jn 20:27.

52. Col 2:9.

53. Jn 1:14.

54. Cf. Gen 6:16.

55. Gen 7:6.

56. Ps 48:9.

good things of God in the land of the living,[57] though they still labor in the land of the dying. Let them see and long, and yearn and run; for you have become the way by which they go, the truth to which they go, the life for which they go.[58] The way is the example of your lowliness; the truth the pattern of your purity; the life is eternal life.

All these, the way, the truth, the life, you have become for us, merciful Father, sweet Lord, loving Brother. You have become the way, the truth, the life for us your children to whom you have said: "My little children, yet a little while am I with you,"[59] for us your servants to whom you said: "You call me master and Lord, and you do well, for so I am,"[60] for us your brethren whom you bid to go whither we shall see you.[61] O good Father, loving Brother, and sweet Lord, you are all that is good and sweet and loving; the sum of goodness overflows in you. Open yourself to us, that your sweetness may flow forth from you to us, and fill us. Open yourself to me, O you who are the door, so that through you I may by longing love attain sometimes to the place of your wondrous dwelling, even to the house of God,[62] although I am not worthy yet to enter there in full reality.

13. For you have opened your servant's ear sometimes, to hear a little of the voice of that exultation and the songs of those that feast;[63] but beyond that he has not been permitted to proceed. You have good reason, therefore, to be sad, my soul; you have good right to be disquieted within me. But "put your trust in God: for I will yet give him thanks who is the help of my countenance and my God."[64] Open to me, O Lord, so that, although I am a stranger unworthy of enrollment yonder as a citizen, yet nonetheless, I may by your gift be suffered on occasion for a little while to journey there, that I may truly see your glory,[65] and not come out again unless I am thrown out! And if I be found worthy to mount up thither oftener, to stay there sometimes, and to return later, I shall

57. Ps 26:13.   58. Jn 14:6.   59. Jn 13:33.
60. Jn 13:13.   61. Mt 28:7.   62. Ps 41:5.
63. *Ibid.*   64. Ps 41:6f.   65. Ps 62:3.

become known to your citizens, who do not suffer now but dwell there all in joy. Their joy no words can tell, and our fellowship with them is for joy, and joy alone. They will not reckon me a stranger, if you command me sometimes to rest among them for a space, in some part of that house of yours. Lord, my heart is restless and impatient for you;[66] I find no rest for it apart from you.[67]

14. When, therefore, I am driven out of heaven, I am so weary of my life that I am ready sometimes to go down alive into hell[68]— may I never descend there dead!—to find out what is happening there too! But when I find it written on the very threshold that there is nobody in hell who worships you,[69] I curse the place and flee. I hear the weeping and gnashing of teeth within;[70] but please, Lord, do not let me go down there! My eyes are ever looking unto you, O Lord, to you who dwell in the heavens,[71] to your house and to Jerusalem your city, whence you came down to us, and of which you brought with you such a marvellous pattern. Kindled by that, I run back thither often with ardor and desire. If I find you, the door, ajar, I enter in; and well it is for me when that is so. But, if I find it shut, I return, distressed. Debarred from seeing your glory, I am sent back wretched to my own abode compelled to bear my own familiar poverty. O if only I may see, if only I may persevere, if only I may hear some day: "Enter into the joy of your Lord,"[72] and may thus enter in never to come out again! Lord, you are mighty and your truth is all about you.[73] Finish your work and give what you have promised.

---

66. Ps 41:6.

67. This passage represents a text of St Augustine: *quia fecisti nos ad te et iniquietum est cor nostrum donec quiescat in te.—Confessions.*

68. Ps 54:16. 69. Ps 6:6. 70. Mt 8:12.

71. Ps 122:1. 72. Mt 25:21. 73. Ps 88:9.

MEDITATION SEVEN

Longing to see God.

"MY HEART HAS TALKED of you, my face has sought you. Your face, Lord, will I seek. Do not turn away your face from me; do not shun your servant in wrath."[1]

It seems surpassing boldness and effrontery to make comparison between my face and yours, Lord God! For you see and judge the hearts of all men[2] and, if you enter into judgment with your servant,[3] the face of my iniquity can only flee before that of your righteousness.

2. But if, in order to excuse and help my poverty, you should grant me burning love and dutiful humility, then let them flee who hate.[4] I, for my part, should not flee your face. For love is very daring, and humility fosters confidence. I am not conscious of these virtues in myself,[5] yet I avow myself your friend. For, if you ask me: "Do you love me?" as you asked Peter, I shall say plainly, I shall tell you boldly: "Lord, you know all things; you know I want

---

1. Ps 26f. William returns again and again to the theme of "the face of the Lord." e.g. see above, the use of this same psalm verse in *Meditation* 2:9, 3:3. Also, where he speaks of the joy to be found in the face of God (Ps 15:1), *Meditation* 3:2, 6:2; of walking in the light of God's face (Ps 88:16), *Meditation* 3:3; on the face guiding his judgment (Ps 16:2), *Meditation* 3:3; and of hiding in the hidden recesses of the divine face (Ps 30:21), *Meditation* 4:11. See also his *Exposition on the Song of Songs*, numbers 35f., 43, 59, etc. (Cistercian Fathers Series 6), pp. 28f., 33, 47, etc., especially the note on pp. 28f.

2. Prov 24:12.   3. Ps 142:2.   4. Ps 67:2.

5. 1 Cor 4:4.

to love you."[6] And that is as much as to say: "If you ask me the same thing a thousand times, I shall as often make the same reply: You know I want to love you."[7] And that means that my heart desires nothing so much as it desires to love you. I cultivate humility as well, which those who make such definitions[8] call contempt of one's own excellence; but as long as I continue sometimes to accede unthinkingly to certain small suggestions of my own superiority, and fail to shake myself free of them with sufficient speed when they are offered me, then I know quite well I am not really humble.

3. There is another sort of humility—namely, the knowledge of oneself. In that, if I am judged according to what I know about myself, it is, as they say, all up with me, and my appearance before your just tribunal is ill-starred. But, if the fact that my sin is ever before me[9] is adjudged a virtue in your sight, of that I think I am not wholly destitute. For my inward gaze turns so often to the foulness of my sins (even when I do not want to think of them and am intent on better things) that I detest myself because of it. O Lord, what more shall I say about my shame-faced conscience? Whatever it is like, whatever its condition, its whole face so desires yours that it scorns and despises all the things of this life, and even life itself, for the love of your face! It does not care a fig what else it sees, as long as it sees you.

4. Thus, O desire of my eyes, my face seeks you meanwhile. I seek your face and, I implore you, do not turn it from me. Teach me, O eternal Wisdom, by the illumination of your countenance, what is that face of yours, and what is mine. For though I burn with desire to see you face to face, I do not know enough as yet of either yours or mine. I know well enough that, if it was not granted to the apostle Paul in this life to see you face to face,[10] and if your

---

6. Jn 21:15ff.

7. This sentence which is found in the Mazarine manuscript is omitted by Robert Thomas in his edition.

8. St Bernard offers such a definition in his tract *On the Morals of Bishops and Clerics*, 4, 19 (Cistercian Fathers Series 19).

9. Ps 50:5.   10. 2 Cor 13:12.

Beloved Disciple, loving and loved as he was, was not allowed to see you as you are,[11] then a man who hopes and seeks to see you in that way is simply not right in his head.

5. And yet, when I hear David speak like this of face and face, hearing another hope in you, I cannot give up hope. And this is not because I have forgotten who I am, but because my trust is in your tender mercy. Although I make poor progress in my loving, I would not like to love you less than any other lover of yours does. For, though it seems that Moses was denied[12] what David by no means despaired of attaining, David himself sings and chants concerning this same Moses and the other Fathers that "they did not get possession of the land through their own sword, neither was it their own arm that saved them; but your right hand and the light of your face."[13] And of himself he says: "O Lord, in your favor you gave strength to my beauty; you turned your face from me, and I was troubled."[14] Turn then to me, most Sweet One, that face which once you turned away from holy David; and, as he was troubled, so shall I be consoled.[15] Turn to me that face by which, before you turned it from him, you willed to increase his beauty. Let your right hand, and your arm, and the light of your countenance, which gained possession of the land of those Fathers in whom you were well pleased, take possession also of my land.

Indeed I find nobody who speaks and treats so often and with such familiarity about your countenance and your face as David,[16] and I cannot think that he lacked experience of it, seeing that he calls for every judgment that he gives to issue from your face,[17] and looks for it to fill him full with joy.[18] Moreover, when declaring the blessedness of the people that can rejoice in you, he says: "They shall walk, O Lord, in the light of your countenance."[19]

6. How much more purposefully can I walk, O God of my

---

11. 1 Jn 3:2.   12. Ex 33:20.   13. Ps 43:4.

14. Ps 29:8.   15. Ps 70:21.

16. David very frequently employs the terms *facies* and *vultus*, the first some sixty-six times and the latter some twenty times in the course of the psalms.

17. Ps 16:2.   18. Ps 15:11.   19. Ps 88:16f.

heart,[20] when I keep looking to your face, that it may guide my judgment, my conscience giving its full assent! I find then that your face, your countenance, means knowledge of your truth; for it is when your blessed people show you the face of good intention that they rejoice greatly in the Holy Spirit, and keep the feast of the great Year of Jubilee[21] in contemplation and enjoyment of your truth. In the light of that truth, that face, they walk, directing all their goings and doings according to the judgments of your righteousness.[22]

7. The knowledge of you has another face, another countenance. Moses was told concerning this: "You cannot see my face, for no man shall see me, and live."[23] It is to the sight and knowledge of the divine majesty that these words refer. That knowledge is best known in this life by unknowing; the highest knowledge that a man can here and now attain consists in knowing in what way he does not know.[24]

8. And yet, O Lord, though you have made the darkness of our ignorance and human blindness the secret place that hides your face from us, nevertheless your pavilion is round about you,[25] and some of your saints undoubtedly were full of light. They glowed and they gave light,[26] because they lived so close to your light and your fire. By word and example they kindled and enlightened others, and they declared to us the solemn joy of this supreme knowledge of you, for which we look hereafter, when we shall see you as you are, and face to face.[27] Meanwhile, through them the lightnings of your truth have illumined the world, and flashes have shone forth[28] that rejoice those whose eyes are sound; although they trouble and perturb those who love darkness rather than light.[29]

---

20. Ps 72:26.

21. Lev 25:8ff.

22. Ps 118:133, 160.

23. Ex 33:20.

24. We have here a clear affirmation of the "negative way" of knowing God which was taught by Denys. However, it is possible that William took his inspiration directly from St Augustine who said that after trying to grasp God the thing the soul knows best is how it does not know him: *De Ordine*, 2, 16, 44 (PL 32:1015).

25. Ps 17:12.

26. Jn 5:35.

27. 2 Cor 13:12.

28. Ps 76:19.

29. Jn 3:19.

9. For this manifestation of your truth, through whomsoever it comes, is like your sun that you make to shine on the just and the unjust alike.[30] The sun, while ever retaining the purity of its own nature, nevertheless makes use of the substances of things as it finds them. It drys up mud and melts wax. It illumines every eye, whether sighted or blind, but with different effect; the seeing eye sees more when illumined, the blind continues in its blindness. So, too, it was when you, God's Wisdom and Truth's Light, by whom all things were made, came into the world. You enlightened every man coming into the world, but the darkness did not embrace you. But to as many as received you and the light of your truth you gave the power to become the sons of God.[31]

30. Mt 5:45.   31. Jn 1:5ff.

MEDITATION EIGHT

The manifold face of man.
The kiss and embrace of the Bridegroom and Bride.

O SUN OF RIGHTEOUSNESS,[1] in making the
light of your face[2] and the splendor of your truth to shine
before the eyes of all, you invite your bride, whoever she
may be: "Show me your face, my sister!"[3] Forthwith the soul of
goodwill, the soul that has received the news of peace from heaven,[4]
the man who is Christ's brother and whose soul is called his sister,
and is in truth, this soul longs to appear before you in your holy
place[5] just as she is, and in your light see light.[6] If she is a sinner, she
shows you the face of her misery, and seeks for the face of your
mercy. If she is holy, she runs to meet you with the face of her
righteousness, and finds in you a face resembling her own; for you
love all righteousness, O righteous Lord.[7] But the soul that has a
harlot's brow has no desire to blush,[8] and, fleeing from truth, comes
face to face with your most fearful justice. For the human soul turns
to you as many faces as she has dispositions. Yet you, O Truth,
receive them all and, though you adapt yourself to all of them, you
are yourself unchanged. Devout humility finds in you friendly
favor; a burning love finds sweetest fuel for its flames; the lowly
heart's contrition finds in you the righteousness it sought; the
harlot's brow finds itself put to shame.

1. Mal 4:2.   2. Ps 4:7.
3. Song of Songs 2:14; "my sister" comes from 4:9, 10, 12.
4. Lk 2:13f.   5. Ps 62:3.   6. Ps 35:10.
7. Ps 10:8.   8. Jer 3:3.

139

K

2. Thus, O Righteousness supreme, do truth and mercy meet in you,[9] when the righteous soul humbly confesses according to the truth of human righteousness; and the truth of your own righteousness, as righteously, has mercy on the soul that makes this true confession. And when she thus proffers the kiss of a righteous confession, you receive her with the kiss of peace. This is the mutual kiss of bridegroom and of bride. That her face might merit to receive your kiss, O Lord, your face was spat upon. That her face might appear as fair and beautiful, your own was smitten by the hands of men, and bruised with blows from rods. Your face was covered with dishonor in the eyes of men,[10] that hers might be found beautiful and lovely in your sight.[11] Moreover, you prepared for her the laver of your precious blood,[12] so that God's children might be washed in it. You bore fearful things for us; for we had done such fearful things that no face of repentance, no matter how great, could possibly atone for them before the face of utmost righteousness, had not your innocence been added to the things you suffered for our sake, had you not been yourself the Son, whose plea was heard by reason of your godly fear.[13]

3. For my hands, Lord, that did what they ought not, your hands were pierced with nails, your feet for my feet. For my unlawful use of sight and hearing your eyes and ears suffered the sleep of death. Your side was opened by the soldier's spear, that, through your wound, out of my unclean heart might flow at last all that in the long process of disgrace had burned and penetrated into it. Lastly, you died that I might live; and you were buried, so that I might rise. This is the kiss your tenderness bestows upon your bride; this is your love's embrace for your beloved. Unhappy is the soul that has not shared this kiss! Unhappy too the soul that falls from this embrace! The thief's confession on the cross earned him this kiss;[14] Peter received it when the Lord looked on him at the time of his denial, and, going out, he wept most bitterly.[15] And many of those who crucified you were turned to you after your passion, and so united

9. Ps 84:11.   10. Jer 3:30.   11. Song 2:13, 14.

12. Eph 5:26; Tit 3:5.   13. Heb 5:7f.   14. Lk 23:43.

15. Lk 22:61f.

to you in this kiss. In the embrace from which the treacherous disciple fell, Mary, whom seven devils formerly possessed,[16] rejoiced. In this embrace the publicans and sinners were enfolded, whose friend and fellow-guest you had become.[17] It included Rahab, the converted harlot, Babylon that knows you, strangers, Tyre, and the black Ethiopians too.[18]

4. Lord, whither do you draw those whom you thus embrace and enfold, save to your heart? The manna of your Godhead, which you, O Jesus, keep within the golden vessel[19] of your all-wise human soul, is your sweet heart! Blessed are they whom your embrace draws close to it. Blessed the souls whom you have hidden in your heart,[20] that inmost hiding-place,[21] so that your arms overshadow them from the disquieting of men and they only hope in your covering and fostering wings.[22] Those who are hidden in your secret heart are overshadowed by your mighty arms; they sleep sweetly, and in the midst of the clergy[23] look forward joyfully, for they share the merit of a good conscience and the anticipation of your promised reward. They neither fail from faintheartedness, nor murmur from impatience.

16. Lk 8:2.   17. Mt 9:10f.; 11:19.

18. Ps 86:4. In the phrase "Rahab and Babylon," Rahab (the stormy one) means Egypt, as also in Ps 89:10 and Is 51:9. William however takes it as meaning the harlot of Jericho who saved the spies and was an ancestress of our Lord. See Josh 2:6ff.; Mt 1:5. Rahab or Egypt stands for pride and quarrelsomeness; Babylon is named for its idolatry, the corruption of its morals, and its material power. According to Ezekiel (27:12ff.), Tyre was completely given over to commerce; very rich, it was not land prepared for the coming of God. Jeremiah alludes to the color of the skin of the Ethiopians (13:23). Their conquest by the Egyptians put them into contact with the Jews who considered them to be a people who were far from God.

19. Heb 9:4.   20. Ps 39:9.

21. Ps 30:21. William's Latin here is rich with assonance: *In abscondito absconditi illius abscondisti.*

22. Ps 90:4, combined with Ps 16:8 and Ps 30:21.

23. Ps 67:14. The Latin is *inter medios cleros* which would seem to mean as it is translated here "in the midst of the clergy." However, it has been more commonly translated as "among the midst of the lots" or "sheep folds." St Bernard interprets the quote "lots" as meaning the two comings of Christ, and it is possible that William has the same idea.

5. But those who kiss thus, sweetly mingle their spirits,[24] and count it pleasure thus to share each other's sweetness. Receive, O Lord, do not reject my whole spirit that I pour out on you in its entirety, despite the fact that it is altogether foul. Pour into me your wholly fragrant spirit that through your fragrance mine may stink no longer, and the sweet smell of you, Most Sweet, may permeate me ever more and more. This is what happens when we do what you told us to do in your remembrance.[25] You could not have ordained a sweeter or a mightier means to forward the salvation of your sons. This is what happens when we eat and drink the deathless banquet of your body and your blood. As your clean beasts,[26] we there regurgitate the sweet things stored within our memory, and chew them in our mouths like cud for the renewed and ceaseless work of our salvation. That done, we put away again in that same memory what you have done, what you have suffered for our sake. When you say to the longing soul: "Open your mouth wide and I will fill it,"[27] and she tastes and sees your sweetness[28] in the great Sacrament that surpasses understanding, then she is made that which she eats, bone of your bone and flesh of your own flesh.[29] Thus is fulfilled the prayer that you made to your Father on the threshold of your passion. The Holy Spirit effects in us here by grace that unity which is between the Father and yourself, his Son, from all eternity by nature; so that, as you are one, so likewise we may be made one in you.[30]

This, O Lord, is the face with which you meet the face of him who longs for you. This is the kiss of your mouth on the lips of your lover; and this is your love's answering embrace to your yearning bride who says: "My beloved is mine, and I am his; he

24. It is here a question not merely of the commingling of breath but of living spirits, of souls. See the passage in the *Exposition on the Song of Songs* where William more fully develops this: n. 30 (Cistercian Fathers Series 6), pp. 25f.

25. Lk 22:19; 1 Cor 11:25.

26. It is a question here of rumination and only the ruminants were considered to be clean animals (Lev 11). The context here is drawn from Ps 67:11: *animalia tua . . . parasti in dulcedine tua pauperi Deus . . . .*

27. Ps 80:11.   28. Ps 33:9.   29. Gen 2:23.   30. Jn 17:21.

shall abide between my breasts."[31] And again, "My heart has said: 'My face has sought you.' "[32]

6. For, if our soul's face does not seek your face, it is not her natural face,[33] but a beast's face, and a mask. Who would not seek your face? Who will not spend his strength for it? Who will not languish, who will not faint for it? Who will not die? Have mercy, Lord! In seeking for your face I should be dead already of I know not what manner of death, had not your visitation kept the spirit in me.[34]

In your face an enemy, by contrast, finds a fiery oven;[35] a sinner finds the portion of his cup, fetters and flames, sulphur and stormy winds;[36] the proud finds the power that resists the proud,[37] the hypocrite the light of truth that he abhors. And all these, whose consciences are branded each with the face of his own particular evil,[38] present in general the face of unrepentant badness. And you receive them with the face of righteousness that judges righteously; their hatred of uprightness meets your hatred of all sin. Because they proved that they knew not God, you gave them over, O Lord, to a reprobate mind, to do those things that are not fitting,[39] things that it is shameful to mention in your presence.[40] Yet they do them brazenly before your face, showing you no respect. From their lusts and the daughters thereof, and their sins and their sins' sons and grandsons, from all this throng of misdeeds they fashion for themselves as it were with links of iron that long, hard, woeful chain that makes a pleasant clanking now, but binds irrevocably and drags them down to hell from where none will ever praise you.[41] O my God, there there is no hope, from there there is no return. Con-

---

31. William draws his inspiration in this section from the Song of Songs: 2:14; 1:1; 2:6, 16; 1:12.

32. Ps 26:8.

33. By the term "natural" here William wishes to signify that the soul created in the image of God in a certain sense naturally seeks the face of God, its creator.

34. Job 10:12: "Your visitation preserved my spirit." St Bernard speaks also of these "visitations" of the Word; see e.g. *Sermons on the Song of Songs,* 57:2; 74:6 (Cistercian Fathers Series 7, 31).

35. Ps 20:10. 36. Ps 10:7. 37. 1 Pet 5:5.

38. 1 Tim 4:2. 39. Rom 1:28. 40. Eph 5:12. 41. Ps 6:6.

cerning such, I wonder whether, when they are in hell, it will be given them in any way to know how great a good it is to enjoy you. If that is so, I think that hell can hold no greater torment than the lack of seeing you.

But alas and alas, those who have committed fearful crimes will also suffer fearful penalties. Your blood, O Christ, will not avail for the impenitent; rather, they will be counted guilty of your blood[42] which they, by sinning and not repenting, have trodden underfoot.[43] This is the face of your wrath,[44] at the prospect of which the Prophet is filled with dread, trembling for those for whom it waits. As the Apostle says: "A certain fearful expectation of judgment and fiery indignation, which shall devour the adversaries."[45] Lord God, you who are Judge of the quick and the dead,[46] there will be those two flocks on Judgment Day, one on your right hand and one on your left.[47] Between these destinies, these flocks, between the lots of life and death, perdition and redemption, wrath and favor, where shall I find myself?[48]

7. O Truth, Truth, by the glory and the splendor of your face, do not hide it from me.[49] Cause all its beams to shine upon me,[50] that in your light I may see light.[51] May I see how my face looks to you and yours to me, and whether just as the truth is in you, Jesus, so the truth is in me, to put off as regards my former way of life the old man who is corrupted by deceitful desires.[52] I know O Truth, with utter certainty, that I am seeking you; but whether I seek truly, that I do not know.

This, then, is the face I lift to you, the face of my sore plight and my great blindness. For though your comforts do rejoice my soul sometimes,[53] I only know what I have been, and not what I am now. One thing I have desired of the Lord, that I will require[54]— namely that, even as the face of my sore plight is lifted in its anguish up to you, so may your mercy's face shine on me more and more,[55] till it consume entirely my wretchedness and gloom.

42. 1 Cor 11:27.   43. Heb 10:29.   44. Is 51:13; Jer 4:26; 25:37f.
45. Heb 10:27.   46. 2 Tim 4:1.   47. Mt 25:31ff.
48. 1 Pet 4:18.   49. Is 64:7.   50. Ps 143:6.
51. Ps 35:10.   52. Eph 4:22.   53. Ps 93:19.
54. Ps 26:4.   55. Ps 30:17.

MEDITATION NINE

William takes stock of his thoughts and his affections.

THERE IS IN ME, O Lord, so vast and dense a mass of misery, that I can neither analyse it into its component parts, nor get a view of the huge thing in its entirety. The fog of it enwraps me now, as it is wont to do, shrouding the sight of you, O Lord my God, to whom I long to speak, dulling my ears against your voice that I desire to hear. Always it happens thus; my own house, my own conscience, casts me out. Is this the meaning of the words: "Let the wicked be taken away, that he see not the glory of God"?[1] And when, with mental vision thus obscured, I try to grope somehow toward my goal, my ardent longing wearies and grows shattered in the quest, and from your heights I fall back to my depths. I fall from you into myself, and from myself I fall below myself. For, when the motive power of my effort is exhausted, I find myself, like some poor thing of dust, cast from the surface of the earth[2] to be the plaything of the winds, a prey to phantom notions, impulses, and longings as many as the faces of mankind, the minutes in the hours, and the ins and outs of circumstances and events. So, while the face of your goodness is always bent on me to work my good, the face of my misery, bowed ever down to the dull earth, is so enshrouded in the fog of its own blindness that it does not know how to reach your presence. Indeed it cannot do so,

1. Is 26:10.   2. Ps 1:4.

145

save insofar as it can never be hidden from the face of your truth, that sees through everything, whatever its condition.

2. Leaving my gift before the altar,[3] then, and giving myself an angry shake, I kindle the lamp of the Word of God, and in wrath and bitterness of soul[4] I enter the dark house of my conscience, determined to find out whence these shadows and this hateful fog proceed, that come between me and the light of my heart.

Then just look what happens! A kind of plague of flies erupts into my eyes, and almost drives me out of my own house! I go in, all the same, as into something that is mine by right; and straightaway I am met by a cloud of thoughts so impudent, so uncontrolled, so diverse, so confused, that the heart of the man that begat them is powerless to sort them out! I sit down, notwithstanding, for I mean to examine them. I tell them to stand before me, so that I may distinguish them, and their appearance, and the notion each contains, for I intend to assign its proper place in me to each of them. Before I can look at them closely, however, before I can tell them apart, they scatter; and, changing places ceaselessly, they seem to mock at me their judge.

I am indignant now, and angry with myself. I stand up. I am going to take more drastic action now against my thoughts, as king in my own kingdom. I call to mind and summon to my aid those thoughts that formerly I have found sure and stable, thoughts that I drew out of the Savior's wells.[5] He is the judge, and he is the accuser; he is the witness too.

3. I pick out my worst thoughts, the unclean ones, as not deserving to be heard at all, needing no judgment to condemn them, and calling for the penalties of penitence to punish them. Idle and troublesome thoughts I drive away like a swarm of unmannerly flies; but I admit those busy thoughts about my work, to which hearing and expression may reasonably be allowed, and I allot to each of them its proper place and time. The thoughts which the judgments of conscience condemn receive their sentence without a murmur. The idle ones, seeing I mean business and fearing to disturb

3. Mt 5:24.   4. Ezek 3:14.   5. Is 12:3.

the process now in train, take flight or are subdued. The busy thoughts, seeing themselves neglected and of small use when their occasions have been taken away, blush to be reckoned with the idle ones and go away.

4. Having thus dispersed the fog of my thoughts for a little while, I turn my attention to their origin, in order to effect the discipline of my affections. I find that, because of the solitude to which I have fled, their entrances and exits are blocked in regard to the things of the flesh. If, however, I should find these open, I confess my misery; and admit I should look with great suspicion on my frailty. But love, the prince of my affections, by the grace of him who strengthens me,[6] reduces the whole crowd of them to bondage under himself;[7] with firm determination he makes room only for that affection which I seek.[8] He issues laws, he orders their behavior, and sets limits that they may not overpass.[9]

5. All fog dispelled, therefore, I now can look with healthier eyes on you, O Light of truth. All other things excluded, I can shut myself away with you, O Truth, alone. Making the secret place of your face my hiding-place,[10] I speak to you more intimately and in more homely fashion; throwing open to you all the dark corners of my conscience. Shedding the garment of skin that you made for Adam to cover his disgrace and shame,[11] I show myself to you as naked as when you made me,[12] and I say: Lord, here I am, not as you made me, but as I have made myself to be by my apostasy from you. Behold my wounds, new and old. I hide nothing. I expose everything, both your benefits conferred on me and my own bad actions.

6. You created me in your image,[13] and put me in your paradise.[14] You gave me a chosen place among your sons, and from my very childhood, polluted as it was, you have shed the light of your face upon me as a seal.[15] But I, for my part, fled the paradise you gave

6. Phil 4:13.   7. Ps 26:4.   8. 1 Cor 9:27.
9. Job 14:5.   10. Ps 30:21.   11. Gen 3:21. Cf. Mk 10:50.
12. Gen 2:25.   13. Gen 1:27.
14. Gen 3:24 in conjunction with Gen 2:15.   15. Ps 4:7.

me, and in its place I found a drain, and hid myself in that. I kept the
seal of your face in my affection always; but by my actions I
rejected it. For by pursuing my desires and the vanities of my heart
I lost my youth and almost embarked on the way of the flesh.[16]
But, all the same, my spirit always loved you, even when my flesh
neglected you.

7. When I took flight from these, I fled to you,[17] and you delivered me out of the whirlpool of the world. I made a treaty with
you; I swore and I resolved to keep the judgments of your righteousness.[18] You opened to me the arms of your mercy and gathered
me into them; and, while I rested sweetly there, I saw the Day of
Man[19] and longed for it. But, willy-nilly, you sent me away—yet
not away from you. If I forgot my God at any time, if I stretched
my hands out whither I should not, forthwith the secret tormentors
of my conscience, armed with your chastening rod, broke my
soul's bones within me, every one, and sinners wrought upon my
back without.[20] Falling and rising, dying and living again, for a
long time you sustained and held me up.

8. When finally both mind and body failed, and out of the belly
of hell I cried to you,[21] your outstretched hand withdrew me from
the lake of misery.[22] You restored me to my former state, and gave
me the joy of your salvation more fully than before.[23]

9. So was I, Lord, and so I am; I stand before you now in my
entirety. My obvious ills are hidden from neither you nor me; but
there are many others, evident to you, that my forgetfulness and
blindness hide from me. If there is any good in me, there is none
quite unspoiled. The enemy has snatched much of it away from me
or, failing that, has flawed it in some way; though indeed I have
spoilt more things of myself than he has damaged for me. See now
my face before you, Lord, my face of misery, uplifted to your face,

---

16. The Migne edition has here instead of *carnis, canis*, which Thomas retains
in his edition, noting the play on words. However the translation here follows
the Davy edition.

17. Ps 142:9.   18. Ps 118:106.   19. Jer 17:18.
20. Ps 128:3.   21. Jon 2:3.   22. Ps 39:3.
23. Ps 50:14.

Mercy supreme. I do not hide its secret nooks and corners from you; you know, Truth, that this is so. I implore you that it may be the truth that I thus show you. For I fear no one as I fear myself, lest, knowingly or otherwise, I should deceive myself.

10. Do I then not believe you, O my God? Do I not trust you, nor believe in you?[24] Do not let them mock me, putting limits or restrictions on my faith. With heart and mouth, with all I do or write, I offer you, O Light of Truth, my willing and complete assent to everything the Catholic Church believes concerning you. If these are bounds sufficient for my faith, then fill them full; and, if they are not wide enough, then widen them. Concerning hope, however, I am bold to say that I do not truly believe if I hope for something other than that which I believe. You, Lord, are my belief, you are my hope. Give me yourself, and I ask nothing else. But, if I do not love, I do not hope; nor do I love unless I hope. And therefore, Father, since my love is poor, my hope is feeble too. And when that wilts which springs up from the root of faith,[25] the root itself grows weak. Nevertheless, O everlasting Life, my faith and hope and love are set on you.

11. O Fatherland, O Fatherland, that from afar I see and greet, where no bad things are found, but all are good! Concerning the bad things, I know that there the evils I have learned so well from long and wearisome experience do not exist; but as to the good things there, my knowledge is as small as my experience.

Have mercy, Lord! Look, I have run and have made straight for you! Rise up to meet me, then, and see,[26] and let me know mine end and the number of my days, that so I may gain knowledge of what it is I lack.[27]

12. I stand in your faith.[28] I go forward in hope. Poor and a

---

24. The insistent repetition in the Latin text conveys the agitation of William: *num quid non credo te, non credo tibi, non credo in te, Deus meus?* However, we might have here an early expression of a formula which would be adopted by the scholastics to express how the act of faith in various ways attains to God directly.

25. 2 Thess 1:3.   26. Ps 58:5f.   27. Ps 38:5.

28. 1 Cor 16:13.

beggar, I supplicate your love.[29] O Love, O Fire, O Charity, come into us! Be you our leader and our light, the fire that consumes and burns in the repentant sinner, be you our paraclete, our comforter, our advocate and helper in all the things for which we pray. Show us what we believe. Grant that for which we hope. And make our face like to the face of God, that we may say, "My heart has said to you, 'My face has sought you.' "[30]

---

29. Ps 39:18.   30. Ps 26:8.

MEDITATION TEN

The Incarnation and Passion of Christ.

"GOD FORBID THAT I SHOULD GLORY, save in the cross of our Lord Jesus Christ."[1] My turning, my conversion, is to the crucified. His cross is my glory; with it my brow is signed, in it my mind rejoices, by it my life is directed and my death is made dear. Lord, do not let me be despised for this by those who merit to behold you sitting uplifted high upon the throne of your divinity and filling all the earth with majesty. For the mysteries of the condescension of your dealing with mankind also "fill the temple" of all contemplation, however vast it is.[2]

2. Let your holy angels have their own glory in heaven, but let them sometimes share their privilege with us on earth as well; for they in their blessed perfection both love to do us service and find it sweet when, as the Apostle says: "The manifold wisdom of God is made known through the church to the principalities and powers in the heavenly places."[3] May they, therefore, forgive us, Lord, even if sometimes we are led by love of you to yearn to see with them that which with them we love. We do not yet rejoice in perfect charity with them who see what we, as yet, do not deserve to see.

3. May they in your wisdom blissfully contemplate the majesty of your divinity, that was contemplated before our time and will be after. It holds within the present of its own eternity the whole of all that was and all that is to be and, reaching from one end to the other

1. Gal 6:14.   2. Is 6:1.   3. Eph 3:10.

mightily, has further strewn with love our own times too, the
times of your dealing with mankind. It sweetly orders all things for
the sake of the daughters of Jerusalem—that is to say, for souls,
devout but as yet weak. Since their faculties are not yet trained to
contemplate these lofty mysteries, they love to be touched and
moved by the lowliness in which you are made like themselves.
Among these souls my spirit also, Lord, will be taught sometimes
to worship you, who are Spirit, in spirit and in truth,[4] nor will the
flesh oppose my doing so when its desires have ceased or grown less
keen.

4. But in the meantime, since it cannot move as freely as it ought
among things divine, you will dispose its own concerns for it as
sweetly as befits it. For, since I have not yet progressed beyond the
elementary stage of sensory imagination, you will allow and will
be pleased if my still-undeveloped soul dwells naturally on your
lowliness by means of some mental picturing. You will allow her,
for example, to embrace the manger of the newborn babe, to
venerate the sacred infancy, to caress the feet of the crucified, to
hold and kiss those feet when he is risen,[5] and to put her hand in the
print of the nails and cry: "My Lord and my God!"[6] And in all
these things, as Job says, "visiting my beauty, I shall not sin,"[7] when
I worship and adore what I see and hear in my imagination, and
what my hands handle of the Word of life.[8] For I will confidently
assert that in the sweet ordering of your wisdom this grace was
provided for us from all eternity. It was not the least of the chief
reasons for your incarnation that your babes in the Church, who
still needed your milk rather than solid food,[9] who are not strong
enough spiritually to think of you in your own way, might find in

---

4. Jn 4:24.   5. An allusion to Mt 28:9.
6. Jn 20:28.

7. Here William has changed the reading of Job 5:24 from "visiting your
beauty," to "visiting my beauty." He explains this more in his *Exposition on
the Song of Songs*, n. 17: "Certainly it is devout to draw near to God even in
this way; and, as Job says, by thus visiting his beauty in God—that is, thinking
of his likeness to God—a man shall not sin." (Cistercian Fathers 6, p. 14.)

8. 1 Jn 1:1.   9. Heb 5:12.

you a form not unfamiliar to themselves. In offering of their prayers[10] they might set this form before themselves, without any hindrance to faith, while they are still unable to gaze into the brightness of the majesty of your divinity.

5. Therefore, although we know you now no longer according to the flesh,[11] but as you now sit glorified at the Father's right hand in heaven, being made so much better than the angels as you have by inheritance obtained a more excellent name than they[12]—therefore, I say, we make our prayer, present our worship, and offer our petitions to that same flesh of ours, which you have not cast off but glorified and made the footstool of your feet.[13] For David bids us do this when he says: "Adore the footstool of his feet, for it is holy."[14]

O blessed is that temple of the Holy Spirit, in which the memory of Christ uplifted on the cross is ever green, where his blood flows ever fresh to save the faithful, loving soul, in whom the Prophet's prayer: "O deliver me and be merciful unto me,"[15] is ever being answered!

6. For the effect of our redemption is repeated in us as often as we recall it in affective prayer. And, since we cannot do even this as we would, with even greater daring we make a mental picture of your passion for ourselves, so that our bodily eyes may possess something on which to gaze, something to which to cleave, worshiping not the pictured likeness only, but the truth the picture of your passion represents.

7. For when we look more closely at the picture of your passion, although it does not speak, we seem to hear you say: "When I loved you, I loved you to the end.[16] Let death and hell lay hold on me, that I may die their death;[17] eat, friends, and drink abundantly, beloved, unto life eternal."[18] And in this way your cross becomes to us like the linen sheet that was shown to blessed Peter, let down from

---

10. *Sacrificium orationis.* William employs the same expression in his *Golden Epistle* n. 64, and in his *Commentary on the Epistle to the Romans* (PL 180:637C).

11. 2 Cor 5:16.	12. Heb 1:3f.	13. Ps 109:1.
14. Ps 98:5.	15. Ps 25:11.	16. Jn 13:1.
17. Cf. Rev 20:13.	18. Cf. Song 5:1.	

heaven by four corners. All sorts went into it, clean creatures and unclean[19]; and we rejoice that we are lifted up to heaven, where also we, who were unclean, are cleansed.

For through this picturing of your passion, O Christ, our pondering on the good that you have wrought for us leads us forthwith to love the highest good. That good you make us see in the work of salvation, not by an understanding arising from human effort nor by the eyes of our mind that tremble and shrink from your light, but by the peaceful experience of love, and by the good use of our sight and enjoyment of your sweetness, while your wisdom sweetly orders our affairs. For he labors who would go up some other way,[20] but he who enters by you,[21] O Door, walks on the smooth ground and comes to the Father, to whom no one may come, except by you.[22] And he no longer labors to understand knowledge beyond his reach,[23] for the bliss of a well-disposed conscience absorbs him utterly. And as the river of joy floods that soul more completely,[24] she seems to see you as you are.[25] In sweet meditation on the wonderful sacrament of your passion she muses on the good that you have wrought on our behalf, the good that is as great as you yourself are great, the good that is yourself. She seems to herself to see you face to face[26] when you thus show her, in the cross and in the work of your salvation, the face of the ultimate Good. The cross itself becomes for her the face of a mind that is well-disposed toward God.

8. For what better preparation, what happier arrangement could have been made for the man who wanted to ascend to his God, to offer gifts and sacrifices[27] according to the precepts of the Law, than that, instead of going up by steps to the altar,[28] he should walk calmly and smoothly over the level of his own likeness, to a Man like himself, who tells him on the very threshold: "I and the Father are one."[29] And he is forthwith gathered up to God in love through

---

19. Acts 10:11f.   20. Jn 10:1.   21. Jn 10:2, 9.
22. Jn 14:6.   23. Eph 3:19.   24. Ps 45:5.
25. 1 Jn 3:2.   26. 1 Cor 13:12. 27. Heb 5:1.
28. Ex 20:26.   29. Jn 10:30.

the Holy Spirit and receives God coming to him and making his abode with him,[30] not spiritually only but corporeally too, in the mystery of the holy and life-giving body and blood of our Lord Jesus Christ.

9. This, Lord, is your face towards us and our face towards you, full of good hope. Deck me with this in your salvation,[31] conform me to this face of your Anointed, for you cannot turn that face away whenever it appears before you in your holy place.[32] Go, man, whoever you are who find this treasure hidden in the field of your own heart![33] Sell all that you have,[34] sell yourself as a slave forever,[35] that you may gain this treasure for your own![36] For then you will be blest and all will be well with you.[37] Christ in your conscience is the treasure that you will possess.

---

30. Jn 14:23.
32. Ps 62:3.
34. Mt 19:21.
36. Lev 25:46.

31. Ps 131:16.
33. Mt 13:44.
35. Perhaps an allusion to Ex 21:6.
37. Ps 127:2.

MEDITATION ELEVEN

He lays bare his blindness,
desiring God to give him light,
and let him lay aside his pastoral charge.

"TURN US AGAIN, O God of Hosts: show your face, and we shall be saved."[1] Thanks to your gift of grace, O Lord, my heart's face is not turned to fleshly things, for you have put all these behind my back, together with the world and all that goes with it. Why then is it, pray, that when in my whole-hearted search for you I have at last discerned your face, whichalone my own face desires, I find myself forthwith cut off from you? Why do you hide your face? Do you account me as your enemy? Do you wish to consume me for the sins of my youth?[2] Is it that I am not yet turned to you, or that you, Lord, are thus far turned away from me? Turn me, O God of Hosts, if I am not turned, and turn to me, O God, if you are turned away,[3] for you have said: "If you will return, O Israel, return to me."[4] And again: "Turn unto me and I will turn to you."[5] You know the gift of grace that is in your poor servant's heart: "O God, my heart is ready, my heart is ready."[6] Command what you will, and make me to understand your command. As you have given me the will to do it, so also give the power; and in me and concerning me your whole will shall be

---

1. Ps 79:8.
2. Job 13:24, 26.
3. Ps 79:8; perhaps also Jer 31:18.
4. Jer 4:1.
5. Zech 1:3.
6. Ps 107:2 or Ps 56:8.

done.[7] I have set my will to do your will, O God, and I embrace with all my heart your law in your commands.[8]

2. You have another law, however, an undefiled law converting souls;[9] and that I do not know, for it is hidden in the secret place of your face,[10] whither I may not enter. If you would grant me entrance there just once, that I might see that law, then with the pen of that swift scribe,[11] the Holy Spirit, I should write it twice and three times on my heart, so that I might have somewhere to return to and, understanding what I was about, might then go straight ahead with confidence and with simplicity.[12] But I am groping in the noonday like a blind man now;[13] in whatever direction I decide to move, I go in fear of pitfalls and destruction. And, like a blind man I am told to go hither or thither, by this way or by that, while I myself, just like a sightless person, do not know in what direction I am travelling, nor by what road I go. Send out to me, O Lord, your light and truth; they have led and brought me to your holy hill and to your dwelling.[14] "I am the way," you tell me, "by which you shall go; I am the truth to which you shall go; I am the life for whose sake you shall go.[15] Whither to go you know, the way also you know."[16] And I, Lord, do not know whither I am travelling, and how can I know the way?[17] You have held me by my hand and led me in your will.[18] You held my hand when you stretched out yours to me, blind as I was and crying after you with tears, and said: "Come unto me, all you who labor and are heavy laden; and I will refresh you."[19]

7. See above *Meditation* 5:7, p. 121, for a parallel passage and the note indicating William's source.

8. Ps 39:9.   9. Ps 18:8.

10. Ps 30:21.   11. Ps 44:2.

12. Prov 10:9. Here begins a certain amount of autobiography which William has woven into this *Eleventh Meditation*. William as he wrote this was still Abbot of St Thierry but he already had a great desire to enter the Order of Cîteaux. He hesitated and sought counsel but the counsel he received did not throw any real light on the situation for him.

13. Deut 28:29.   14. Ps 42:2.   15. Jn 14:6.

16. Jn 14:4.   17. Jn 14:5.   18. Ps 72:24.

19. Mt 11:28.

3. Since I heard that, I have run the way of your commandments, for you have set my heart at liberty.[20] I came to you, O God, and I offered you my heart, my ready heart,[21] saying: "What will you have me to do?"[22] And you replied: "Go, sell all that you have and give to the poor, and come and follow me."[23] I went, I ran, I sold all that I had, even my body and my soul; I gave nothing to the poor, because I possessed nothing. I sold to you, O Lord, all that I had, and you are my reward. You know that I have kept nothing for myself; if there is anything that has escaped me and still lies hidden in some secret corner of my conscience, I will search it out and faithfully offer it to you. But when I ask you to repay me, you charge me with the offences of my youth,[24] an ancient debt. Have patience with me, Lord,[25] I beg you, for I have not the wherewithal to pay you back. I have come thus far, and now here I stand; I may go no further.[26]

4. A poor blind beggar sitting beside the road along which you are going, I cry to you: "Son of David, have mercy on me!" The crowds bear down on me, rebuking me, telling me to be quiet.[27] But I cry out so much the more: "Have mercy on me, Son of David!"[28] I am weary from crying, my throat is hoarse, my sight fails me for waiting so long upon the living God;[29] but you pass by him who cries to you.

5. Sometimes you stand still for me, but only for a little. You tell me to come to you, and you say: "What do you want me to do for you?"[30] I say, and all my bones say with me:[31] "Lord, that I may

20. Ps 118:32.   21. Ps 107:2 or also Ps 56:8.

22. Acts 9:6. The attraction to enter the Order of Cîteaux was for him a second vocation. He answered this new call of the Lord but he did not have any longer any goods to give to the poor.

23. Mt 19:21.   24. Ps 24:7.   25. Mt 18:26.

26. Job 38:11. St Bernard did not judge it opportune for William to transfer from St Thierry to Clairvaux.

27. This is perhaps an allusion to the opposition which came to William's project from his fellow Benedictines.

28. Mk 10:46ff.   29. Ps 68:4.

30. Mk 10:49ff.   31. Ps 34:10.

see!" Yet you pass on. Have mercy on me, Son of David! I cannot follow you, for I am blind. Have mercy on me! From you I had whatever little motive power there was that drew me towards you, but I have not sufficient power to run after you. Have mercy on me, Son of David, have mercy on me! Have mercy on me, you at least, my masters[32] and the servants of God and say to him: "Send him away, for he cries after us."[33] Woe is me that my sojourning is prolonged! My soul has been for long a sojourner in the house of darkness.[34] What have I done? What have I achieved? It is the Lord. He will do what he sees to be good.[35]

I will sit beside the road, I will not leave the road.[36] Maybe he will come back sometime without the crowds, and see me, who myself do not see, and pity me. For in my heart I treasure a good word of his: "Wait for the Lord, do manfully, and let your heart be comforted and hold fast to the Lord."[37]

6. Gather yourselves meanwhile,[38] my soul and all my inward parts;[39] "the Word of God is living and effective. Sharper than any two-edged sword, it pierces even to the dividing asunder of soul and spirit and of the joints and marrow, and is a discerner of the thoughts and intents of the heart. Neither is any creature unseen in his sight; all my concerns are naked and open to his eyes."[40] "I said unto the Lord: 'You are my God, my lots are in your hand,' "[41] expresses the same thing. Let us have done, then, with the lot, which entailed the sin which has brought on us this evil[42] that God should turn away his face from his own child![43] The purpose of my

---

32. Job 19:21. William has transposed the "at least you my friends" of Job to "my masters" wishing to speak especially of his Benedictine co-abbots.

33. Mt 15:23.

34. Ps 119:5f. William has replaced the "cedar" with *domus tenebrarum*.

35. 1 Sam 3:18.   36. 2 Pet 2:15.

37. Ps 26:14. St Bernard did not definitively close the doors of Clairvaux to William; he, however, demanded that he should wait, think, and pray.

38. An allusion to Gen 49:1. William takes counsel with himself. He is troubled and he asks himself if he has done well in taking steps to free himself from the burdens of the abbatial office in order to become a Cistercian.

39. Ps 102:1.   40. Heb 4:12f.

41. Ps 15:2; 30:16.   42. Jon 1:7.   43. Ps 68:18.

lot is the finding of your truth, O God. As the Lord lives,[44] if my right hand, my eye or my foot offends me, I will not spare it; I will cut it off and cast it from me.[45] Tell me, O Word of God, can it be that I have not done well in trusting you so wholly as to leave all and follow you?[46] My every thought, all the intents of my heart, my soul and my spirit, my joints and my marrow[47] answer, "Yes, you have done well!"[48] I go on to enquire: "Was this good act perhaps ill-done?" My thoughts whisper the answer and say, when they are given leave to speak: "The Lord said to Peter: 'Do you love me?' He answered: 'You know that I love you,' and was bidden, 'Feed my sheep.' "[49] Three times he said it, that it may be seen a threefold cord cannot be lightly broken.[50] For love's proof lies in shepherding the flock.

7. *Intents:* A shepherd who is not a hireling, even though he lays down his life for the sheep, scarcely meets all their needs.[51] But it is a very serious thing for him to be in charge of the flock, when he cannot give it profitable service. There was a time when David the king was so weak in body that he took to his bed, so chilly from old age that no coverings could warm him.[52] And from his bed he had to rule God's People by his word alone, and the eyes of all Israel looked to him in all things.[53] Bewitchment with trifles did not as yet obscure the good;[54] the stubborn wickedness of a decadent age

---

44. A Biblical expression which occurs frequently in the accounts of Elijah, see 2 Kings 2:2, 4, 6, etc.

45. Mt 18:8f.   46. Lk 5:11.

47. Heb 4:12f. Drawn no doubt by the opening of this passage in Hebrews: "Let us therefore strive to enter that (God's) rest," William structures the rest of this *Meditation* upon it, calling upon the various elements, Intent of the Heart, the Joints, the Marrow, the Spirit, and the Soul to confirm in dialogue his response to the searching Word of God in regard to his desire "to enter that rest." The "Joints" to some extent play the role of the defender of the bond while the "Marrow" quite aptly pleads for the deep inner life.

48. This he says in reference to his desire to resign.

49. Jn 21:17.   50. Eccles 4:12.

51. Jn 10:11 in connection with Jn 15:13.

52. 1 Kings 1:1.   53. 1 Kings 1:20.

54. Wis 4:12.

had not then reached such a pitch as to withhold its respect from old men of proven worth.[55]

8. But now, although the church's shepherds have to feed the Lord's flock in body and soul at once—for all the Lord accounts the soul as more important, saying: "Seek first the kingdom of God," and frees his ministers from care for the body, as secondary, saying further: "And all these things shall be added unto you,"[56]—in spite of all this, I say, who would listen to anyone who preached thus today? Who would let him practice it? Who would have any consideration for the old man? Who would make allowances for the weak? The wisdom of the flesh, the spirit of this world, a zest for knowledge, elegance of manner, and the like are required today of those who control the church. Simplicity is mocked, religion is despised, humility is held to be of no importance. And whereas hitherto it has seemed sufficient if a person in authority was competent in the administration of interior goods, who is there today for whom this is enough, unless there are plenty of exterior goods as well?

And O that a superior might know his own limitations! Woe is us for this, for we have sinned.[57] Because of this, as the Prophet says: "We have given the hand to Egypt and to Assyria, to be satisfied with bread."[58] For, in contradiction to the Apostle's teaching, "we have become the servants of men,"[59] of thieves and usurers, the sons of strangers abounding in the riches of this world. If a superior is not obedient to the nod of such as these today, if he does not conform himself to the world that is fashioned on these lines, if he does not cringe to those set over his head[60] and flatter his

55. A bit of bitterness seems to assault here William's accustomed sweetness. The fact that while still at St Thierry he could already consider himself an old man (and therefore at least approaching his sixties) makes his relationship with the younger Bernard (who would have been perhaps a full twenty years younger) all the more interesting.

56. Mt 6:33. St Benedict presents the same doctrine concerning the role of the Abbot and employs the same Scripture texts. See RB 2:35.

57. Lam 5:16.   58. Lam 5:6.   59. 1 Cor 7:23.

60. An accommodation of Ps 65:10 which St Benedict also employed in his fourth step of humility: RB 7:41.

subjects, making pretence of much and concealing even more,[61] what will he do? What can he do? Where will he find himself? For today even compliance makes only a few friends, and those unsure and undependable; and truth makes open, cruel, and persistent enemies.

9. If only this may really be the way by which we lay down our life for the brethren![62] If only the outward covering of goat's hair curtains may so absorb the buffeting of this wind, that the house of God within may abide in its beauty![63] And O that the sword may not reach to the soul![64] For we have grown benumbed by the bewitchment of trivial matters[65] and the importunity of desire, and our hearts have got hardened;[66] we are become as Ephraim, a heifer taught to tread out corn.[67] Thus we have departed from ourselves; thus have our heart's interests been transferred to unavoidable tasks; so that we, whose duty requires us only to perform them, take pleasure in doing things that ought to make us feel nothing but shame and disgust. Yes, and even those on whom such tasks are not laid strive after this same pleasure! Where today is Martha, with her complaint that she is left to serve alone?[68] Is it not Mary's grumble that is heard all over the house today, because she is permitted to sit at the Lord's feet?[69]

Having endangered both our body and our soul by a long service and a diminution of our resources through prolonged labors, it is right, as we assert, for us now to look to the hands of the royal munificence, that it may allow our old age recognition of its deserts, and bestow on it a better thing than that which it itself is conscious of

---

61. In the Latin there is a play here on words: *simulando ... dissimulando*.

62. 1 Jn 3:16.

63. An allusion to Ex 26:7ff. where the make-up of the tabernacle for the Ark of the Covenant is described. An outer tent of goat's hair was to protect the inner tent of fine colored linen. It was for the superiors to care for the outer thing so that the ordinary monk and nun might be left safe within to glorify God in the beauties of contemplation.

64. Jer 4:10.   65. Wis 4:12.

66. This is a Biblical expression which is found frequently, especially in Exodus, as a description of Pharoah: 7:13, 22, etc.

67. Hos 10:11.   68. Lk 10:40.   69. Lk 10:39, 42.

deserving. Must Jacob always put up with his blear-eyed Leah? Must he always serve for Rachel, and never get her?[70] Moreover Jacob was required to surrender all his transitory goods,[71] since his wages were changed every day,[72] so that he should get the black instead of the white. At home he had his wives consumed with jealousy,[73] abroad was Laban, girding at him with his sons.[74] Jacob must set his own house in order some time,[75] and it seems only right that now at last, when he is old and failing, he should be allowed to go back to his father's home.[76]

10. *Joints:* If the matter begins thus, so will it end. For the joints are dislocated all over the body; and, since the body's unity is lost and parts[77] are forming, it must needs fall to pieces. The divided kingdom will be laid waste,[78] and one house will fall upon another.

A wise father of a family, when he is about to set out on a pilgrimage and is setting his house in order and has given to each of his servants authority in some particular task, sets a doorkeeper at the entrance of his house.[79]

11. A house without a doorkeeper is a public lodging-house, where whoever likes comes in and goes out, and brings what he likes inside and takes what he likes away. The house is a Church,[80]

---

70. William here alludes to the ruse which Laban laid on Jacob in giving him in marriage, first of all, his blurry-eyed daughter Leah in place of Rachel. In the patristic tradition, Leah, like Martha in the New Testament, is a type of an active fruitfulness which failed to see the more sublime beauties of the transcendent reality which are seen by the contemplative typified by Rachel and Mary of Bethany. See Gen 29:16ff. and Lk 10:39ff.

71. Gen 31:39.   72. Gen 31:7.   73. Gen 30:14ff.

74. Gen 31:1ff.   75. Gen 30:30.

76. Gen 30:25. Once again Jacob speaks of his old age.

77. *Partes:* to do justice to the word as used by William we would have to translate this as "parts" and also as "parties."

78. Mt 12:25.   79. Mk 13:34.

80. William has in mind here especially that little church which was his monastery. At that time the word "church" did not signify only a place reserved for worship but more the assembly of the brethren whether local or in a monastery. Thus one would speak of "the Church of St Thierry" to designate the abbey.

and the doorkeeper, Christ Jesus, is himself the door.[81] He who either comes in or goes out except by him is a thief; he climbs up or down, by some other way.[82] Christ was made obedient to the Father even unto death.[83] He who does not obediently keep this rule has departed from Christ, as the Apostle says: "Consider him, who endured such contradictions of sinners against himself, lest you be wearied and faint in your minds. For you have not yet resisted unto blood."[84] Old age and weakness excuse no one, till he, who led him in, himself shall lead him out. Otherwise, if there be a door without a doorkeeper, open to all comers, what will ensue but that there shall be equal freedom for all and sundry to go out or come in?

12. *Marrow:* Alas, alas, "the ungodly walk round about; according to your highness, O God, you have multiplied the children of men."[85] Driven around in the circle of error, we become so dizzy and bewildered that we cannot reach the center of truth, the unmoving point of unity which, though itself unmoving, gives movement to the whole. He is the truth; he himself said: "I am the Truth,"[86] and also: "You shall know the truth, and the truth shall make you free"[87]— free, surely, from the circle of error. Let us reflect, therefore, on the center of truth, whether the circle we are pursuing is governed by and through him. By the laws of truth, if our course is truly set it meets itself; if it does not, error is manifest.

13. Let us review our affections and actions. Let our affections be set on the center of truth, and then the outward action will correspond thereto, as the circumference to the center. Every affection is indeed owed to God. When he is adhered to faithfully, wherever the circle of activity revolves, it cannot err from the right but meets itself truly, so that its radius is of equal length at every point. There can be a point without a circle, but in no way can a circle be drawn without a central point.

Affection is sufficient if circumstances do not demand action or the possibility of acting is lacking. For when the demands of love

---

81. Jn 10:7, 9. 82. Jn 10:1. 83. Phil 2:8.
84. Heb 12:3f. 85. Ps 11:9.
86. Jn 14:6. 87. Jn 8:32.

require action, true charity owes it to God or to a neighbor as the case may be; if necessity does not require it, the love of truth makes it our duty to hold ourselves at leisure for itself.[88] And as we always owe our entire affection to God, so also, when we are at leisure, we owe our whole activity to him. And when a neighbor's need does not require it, he who diverts a part of his affection or activity from God commits a sacrilege. But anyone whom necessity does require to act must not be so eager to perform it, that he fails to take stock of his own ability to do it. The center of truth must be consulted as to whether he has the ability or not. If he has not, and yet presumes to act, he is not cleaving to the center, and so he destroys the perfection of the circumference. For there are people who have no love for cleaving to the point of stability; they always want to be circling round outside.

These are the wicked, who go round in a circle; these are the sons of men. When the profundity of God's judgment multiplies them in this present age, or allows them to be multiplied, they become the enemies of unity and truth. This is the end. Let him from whom action is urgently demanded, if indeed he can do so, fix his attention on the truth, and not refuse to do the act of service. If the truth, when it has been consulted, tells him he is unequal to the task and no fit person for it, then let him fix his soul in stillness on the stability of truth, lest, being as it were on the rim of the wheel,[89] he be sent over the precipice of error.

14. But if, when necessity makes urgent claim, a person whom the truth, when consulted, has absolved from meeting it, decides,

---

88. "true charity . . . love of truth"—literally, "the truth of charity . . . the charity of truth." See the same balanced inversion of words and the same development of thought above in William's treatise, *On Contemplating God*, n. 1, p. 36. When William wrote that treatise he was a young Abbot of St Thierry. He then already sensed that when his duties did not hold him fast— the truth of charity—he would resign from the occupations and preoccupations of his charge and the care of the brethren in order to consecrate himself entirely to contemplation—the charity of truth. Nevertheless at least from time to time he was able to forget everything, his worries, his suffering, the services to be rendered, etc., in order to give himself to prayer, to lose himself in God.

89. Cf. Ps 82:1.

without great fear as to his ability, to follow his own will, a great error has him in its toils. For if he errs knowingly, he is guilty both of neglect towards his neighbor and of deception in relation to the truth; he does not perform the action and he lacks the affection. He does not err so much, if he errs unknowingly; but he errs wholly if he thinks it does not matter. He is not, however, wholly a stranger to truth, who does not fear the judgment of truth. Let us, therefore, who must shortly enter into judgment with the truth, avoid all the windings of error by a brief and faithful statement and because perhaps we want not to be able to perform the action, let us confess ourselves as liars according to our own judgment, so that we may not be found liars before the bar of truth. That done, and seeking pardon for both our disposition and our action, we shall appear as tellers of the truth before the bar of truth. For we must not act with guile in the sight of the truth, lest our iniquity be found out and hated.[90]

15. *Spirit:* I agree. And this is indeed the marrow and centre of the truth not to hug one's disease, but to let the poison of one's inward wickedness drain away.

16. *Soul:* That is how the matter stands. As once I took pleasure in being in authority, so now my will is to be in subjection; and my self-will is glad now to have the excuse of my own needs and does not allow me to attend to the needs of the brethren.

17. *Spirit:* Although, O soul, you do not lack a full compassion for the brethren's need, nevertheless your affection is even as you say. Nothing remains, therefore, but humble confession and striving after every virtue, so that, however unfruitful and useless we may appear outwardly, we may not be found wholly barren and empty inside. And although the crowds bear down to silence us, let us cry with our whole heart and mind: "Iesus, Son of David, have mercy on me!"[91]

90. Ps 35:3.

91. Mk 10:47. And so finally William perseveres in his petition for admission into the Order of Citeaux.

MEDITATION TWELVE

Confession of sin
and of longing to love God.

"HEAR MY PRAYER, O Lord, give ear to my supplication in your truth; hear me in your righteousness."[1] Lord, you who are near to all who call on you in truth, according to the promise made to us in the Scripture of your truth.[2] Even as the truth is present with yourself, my will is set to call on you in truth today. Hear me therefore, O Truth, in the multitude of your mercy and in the truth of your salvation.[3] For I said: "Now I have begun. Be this your change, O right hand of the highest."[4] For my past sins and evils, which are great, inveterate and numberless, have made me vile and despicable to myself.[5] And, as to my good qualities, if any such have been observed in me, I am most suspicious of them.

2. Therefore I come to you today, as one whose whole past life is dead; so that in you, O Fountain of new life, I may begin again. If I have done any good things, they are yours. To you I hand them over; do you return them to me in your own good time.[6] The bad things that I have committed are my own; alas, how many and how great they are, and most of them have slipped my memory!

O that a suitable repentance may efface from your remembrance, too, the sins whose horror is such that no forgetfulness can ever wipe them out of my memory! I so detest their memory that I

1. Ps 142:1.   2. Ps 144:18.   3. Ps 68:14.
4. Ps 76:11.   5. Job 7:20.   6. Ps 68:14.

frequently wish that I had forgotten all of them completely long ago. But please, Lord, do not you remember the transgressions of my youth.[7] They were the Egyptian firstborn, whom you destroyed in Egypt.[8] When I came out of Egypt,[9] I left Egyptian deeds behind.

3. For a long time after that you led me through the wilderness, and taught and kept me as the apple of your eye;[10] you rebuked me when I sinned, in grief you gave me comfort, and you instructed my ignorance until you brought me to the very threshold of the promised land.[11] When I stand there, beholding the delights of "the land of the living"[12] that you show me, and then remember what was said to Moses: "You shall see it, but you shall not enter it,"[13] then my whole being is convulsed with dread. If he deserved to hear those words for committing a single sin, what shall I hear, who have today so many and such great transgressions to wipe out before you?

4. And yet, O Truth, just as all my past misdeeds, whether remembered or not, and all the chastisement which they merit, which is not past, are in your sight even when I say not a word, even so let them come today before your eyes as I confess them to you. Let them be gathered in a single bundle to be burnt;[14] it will be an enormous faggot too, and more than I can carry if there is nobody to help![15] I do not specify or make a list of them, nor am I able to; but howsoever much and in whatever way I have in truth sinned before you, O Truth, I own myself to be the sinner that you know I am. Let nobody make light of my misdeeds to me, nor yet

7. Ps 24:7.   8. Ps 134:8.

9. The topology which compares conversion to monastic life with the Exodus is common among the Cistercian Fathers. See for example Aelred of Rievaulx's *Sermons for the Feast of St Benedict*, trans. M. B. Pennington in *Cistercian Studies*, 4 (1969) pp. 62–89, and the introduction and notes there.

10. Deut 32:10.

11. For William here the land of Egypt is the world; the desert, the monastic life among the Benedictines which he had been living; the promised land or "the land of the living" was for him at this time the Order of Cîteaux. William longed to be admitted into that new, flourishing and fervent monastic community.

12. Num 27:12; Ps 26:13.   13. Deut 32:52.

14. Mt 13:13.   15. Ps 21:12.

exaggerate; let no one make them out as either less or more, not even I myself. Before you, O God, I stand for trial. I will not spare myself, O Lord, you spare me.[16]

5. Yet do not spare me in such a way as from this day to reckon me your enemy,[17] and to write bitter things against me, and cause me to be brought to nought amid the sins of my past life.[18] Keeper of men, do not any longer count me as your adversary, for being such has made me a grievous burden to myself, but rather take away the sin[19] that comes between yourself and me.[20] If you do pardon, Lord, then pardon me; if it pleases you to punish, then I myself will be your fellow-punisher. But do not bruise me with your blows, as though you were my enemy,[21] for I am ready to accept the scourge from your hand, and my grief shall be ever in your sight. I will tell out my iniquity and remember that I am suffering for my sin.[22] For I am not handing myself over into the hands of an enemy; I am committing myself with complete trust into yours, of which so often I have had experience. When one of your hands strikes me, the other one caresses; and when one knocks me down, the other catches me, so that I am not bruised. But there are times when, in an anger greater than that of enemies, you stretch out your hand,[23] times when you turn your face away from us in wrath.[24] You strike harder then than any enemy, and then the heavens become as brass to us, and the earth iron,[25] and everything is hard and everything is evil; for that is what always happens when your face is turned away. For your name's sake, O Lord, spare your servant in this; flog us as much as you like, as long as the light of your face shines always upon us, and you have mercy on us![26]

Nevertheless, you are the Lord of vengeance,[27] remitting it or mitigating as you will. For you have turned our evils on yourself[28] and, paying in your Passion the things you did not take,[29] you have

---

16. Joel 2:17.   17. Job 13:30.   18. Job 13:26.
19. Job 7:20f.   20. Is 59:2.   21. Jer 30:14.
22. Ps 37:18f.   23. Ps 137:7.   24. Ps 87:15.

25. Deut 28:23. William uses the same image in his *Exposition on the Song of Songs*, n. 201 (Cistercian Fathers 6), p. 161.

26. Ps 66:2.   27. Ps 93:1.   28. Ps 20:12.   29. Ps 68:5.

prepared your throne for judgment;[30] so that, having been unjustly
judged yourself, you may in justice absolve the justly judged.

6. Your judgments then shall help me, Lord.[31] You shall look on
me according to the judgment of those who love your name,[32] even
as you once passed judgment on the sinful woman who loved you,
saying: "Her many sins are forgiven, for she loved much."[33] May
your own love be my advocate today in this my cause; if I shall
have refused it on earth, I fear lest it may refuse me in heaven.[34] If
here I have been ashamed to own you, there you will be ashamed of
me.[35] I am ashamed—because my love is not what it ought to be.
And, because today is my judgment day, do you, Judge of my heart,
judge me today also in this respect, and sift my cause[36] to see whether
in fact I have the advocate I claim. For in this matter my spiritual
sight is so darkened, that I am entirely uncertain whether I seem to
myself to see what I do not see, or not to see what I do really see.

Now most assuredly it seems to me that I always love your love,
insofar as I am moved by it whenever I think of it or am reminded
of it. But when this does not happen, when I think of you or am
reminded of you and am not moved or touched, I fear that perhaps
this fact of my unmovedness convicts me of not always loving you,
for the signs of your most present power and goodness strike and
arouse the dullness of my perceptions everywhere and on every side.

7. O Light of Truth, dispel these shadows from me today and drive
away the fog! Feed me with the bread of life and understanding,
and give me the water of wisdom to drink![37] Indeed to understand
your mysteries is both food and drink, for they are the things we
work and labor at, taking hold of them, and as it were chewing
them. But some of them, like drink, go through us as they are, and
refresh us in their own way.[38]

---

30. Ps 9:8.   31. Ps 118:175.   32. Ps 118:132.   33. Lk 7:47.
34. Mt 10:33.   35. Lk 9:26.   36. Ps 42:1.   37. Sir 15:3.

38. See St Gregory's homilies on Ezekiel, Book 1, 10, 3: "The Holy
Scripture is our food and our drink. . . . sometimes food, sometimes drink.
For the more obscure passages which can be understood only if they are
explained are food, for all that which explains them is, as it were, chewing
which must take place first in order that we might swallow it. But the more
clear passages, they are our drink, for we can swallow them without chewing."

For when we seek your love by means of understanding, and sometimes find it, that is the very bread of life that strengthens the heart of man.[39] This bread we often seek with great labor before we get it, for the penalty of Adam's sin is that we should eat our bread in the sweat of our face.[40]

But sometimes your Spirit blows where and when he will and breathes on us the favor of your love. We hear his voice, because we receive the feeling of love, but we do not know by what judgment of your mercy it comes,[41] nor by what judgment of your justice it passes us by, as it were with only a greeting, sometimes with more sweetness, sometimes with more violence. This is drink. Feed me, O Lord, today with your bread that gives life to the world.[42] With regard to these questions that I ask about your love, may a more firm and solid understanding be given me. And may the sweetness of your grace as a wholesome drink arrange and soften this food lest a more solid food harm my feeble senses rather than strengthen them.

8. I ask, O Lord, whether I have your love. If I find that I have, that is the only claim to praise my soul can make,[43] and I am glad of it. But if I have not got it then my soul is hateful to me, and there is nothing that I love, seeing I hate myself. I perceive and acknowledge that I have the love of your love, insofar as I would love nothing whatever, not even myself, except in and for your love. If only I might be found fully worthy to behold its face, to walk openly in its light, and to enjoy its pleasures, I would not mind at all how I gave myself for it, either in death or life.

This is the witness of my conscience, when I call it out and examine it in the light of your truth; it seems to me to answer boldly about the love of your love. But in regard to you as to whether it always loves you and loves you enough, it is afraid to answer in your judgment. Certainly, wherever I see your love and the patent signs of it, I am wholly glad; but, although all things on

39. Ps 103:15.
41. Jn 3:8.
43. Ps 33:3.

40. Gen 3:19.
42. Jn 6:33.

M

all sides are always bearing witness to me of the presence of your goodness and power, I am sometimes scarcely moved by this.

9. If, then, you ask me today, as once you asked the blessed Apostle: "Do you love me?" I hesitate to answer: "You know I love you,"[44] but I do readily and with a clear conscience make reply: "You know I want to love you."[45] Lift up my eyes, O Lord, and I will ponder all the marvels of your law,[46] the law of your love.

Perhaps the reason why I believe that I love your love is that, as often as I think of you and it, I do to some extent perceive and see and taste it, whereas perception of yourself is wholly or almost wholly lacking to me. With sight it is the same, and I have only a very rare and meager taste of you. That which is not known directly to the lover is loved only with difficulty. Your great and frequent kindness and your love itself, which I most surely love, send me to you; but, when I do not find you, I fall back on your love and, not without hope, repose in it.[47] For when I sweetly perceive your love, I seek you yourself by understanding that love. I love what I perceive, I long for what I seek, and I languish in my longing. For even if occasionally the understanding itself is by your gift affected to some small extent, it still is not allowed to have the full taste of the good savor that it has perceived.[48] This is as it were snatched out of its mouth, so that it falls back into its previous state of hunger and ignorance, and is not allowed to remain in the light of your countenance till in your light it can discern and put an end to this harrowing uncertainty.

10. When in my meditation the fire kindles[49] and I try to find out what I have, and what I lack,[50] asking your help in the matter I begin to make a staircase for myself, by which I may ascend to you. The

---

44. Jn 21:17. The Apostle here is St Peter.

45. William returns here to the distinction between love and loving or wanting to love.

46. Ps 118:18.   47. Ps 15:9.

48. He is speaking here of the knowledge that comes from love, from the experience of God, of the love that becomes knowledge by the inspirations of the gift of wisdom.

49. Ps 38:4.   50. Ps 38:5.

steps of it, that I set up for myself in my heart, are these: first, a great will is needed, then an enlightened will, and thirdly, a will upon which love has laid its hand. Everyone who mounts up to you needs first this great will, great as he can make it. He also needs a will enlightened by your gift and moved in your own way—a will that is as great as you created it, enlightened as far as you have made it worthy to receive your light, and moved according to the form that you have given it.

However, you have formed without form, for, since you are neither form nor anything that has been formed, so neither can your love have any form in such a way as that it should be formed in anything, as something formed. For your love is the Wisdom of which it is said, "It is the breath of the power of God and a certain pure overflowing of the glory of almighty God, and therefore no defiled thing can come upon it. For it is the brightness of the everlasting light and the unspotted mirror of God's majesty, and the image of his goodness."[51] Wherefore we cannot apprehend it as we wish. Unless it first comes to us and its favor precedes us, the effort of our understanding, whatever it be, avails us little or nothing. For as the Apostle says, you are "in the form of God."[52] The form of your Godhead is the very simplicity of your nature and substance, and its love must be like it. A certain wise man says in regard to faith in you: "We ought to try to believe in a thing as it actually is."[53] So all the more should this be so in regard to love in so far as charity surpasses faith. It is the heart alone that discerns this.

11. My will towards you is such that I can have no greater; and I would rather not exist at all, than be without it. Had not the protection of this shield encircled me of old,[54] when men rose up against me, they might well have swallowed us alive.[55] I have indeed at times felt some sweet urgings of illuminating grace[56] and affective charity; but the experience of their fullness is far removed from me. And because by reason of my sins such will as you have

---

51. Wis 7:25f.

53. Boethius, de Trinitate, II: PL 64:1250A.

55. Ps 123:2f.

52. Phil 2:6.

54. Ps 5:13.

56. See above, p. 39, n. 25.

given me is seldom and but little enlightened and still more rarely affected, and because in this matter my desires and deserts accord so ill, I do not know whether I ought to call it love.

12. Those who make definitions define love as only a certain intense will; but they can form no judgment on the limits of your love. If it be called desire, I agree; for in very truth I do desire you. But as long as my conduct appears so poor and wretched before you, my conscience can have no joy. Let him who will, laugh and mock at me; I know what I am suffering in this matter. I know that no one shares my suffering in this who has not suffered or is not suffering the same. "My tears shall be my meat day and night, while they daily say to me, 'Where is now your God?' "[57]—that is, as long as there is any affection in my soul in which, after his own fashion, my God is not. And especially is this the case with love, which ought to be his special abode in me. He will not rid me of this grief till he reveals himself to me, when I will see what I love, and love with unperturbable joy what I see. But in the meantime I love in part what I in part perceive; and if I did not to some extent perceive it, I should not love it at all.

13. For when I see your children feasting at your table, amid the delights of your love, for all that I myself am starving I love your love in them intensely, and in my heart I do embrace most tenderly those who love you thus. And I see them rejoicing in my joy which joy I have because of theirs. And I see that they want to express the measure of their joy, but cannot do so. For the affection that they enjoy in loving you can indeed be perceived in the sensible sweetness of a certain spiritual or divine joy; but, just as the savor of any sort of food can penetrate nobody unless he tastes of it, so can that savor neither be examined by reason, nor explained in words, nor yet perceived by the (bodily) senses. It is something divine, the pledge and the betrothal gift of the Spirit,[58] by means of which you, God, rejoice and feed your poor servant in this life, lest he should faint by the way.[59] And in regard to the joy of life eternal, as Job says: "You tell your friend that it is his, and that he can reach it."[60]

57. Ps 41:4. 58. 2 Cor 1:22. 59. Mt 15:32. 60. Job 36:33.

14. For the holy soul is refashioned in the image of the Trinity, the image of him who created her[61] after the very manner of his own beatitude. For just as we say and believe of the Trinity that there are three Persons, so also the enlightened and affective will— that is, understanding and love and the disposition of enjoyment— are three personal affections, in a sort of way; but the substance of beatitude is one, for nothing is loved except by being understood, nor understood except by being loved, and when a man is found worthy to enjoy a thing he does not do so unless he also both loves and understands it.

To have and to enjoy, then, is to understand and love. Happy is the conscience whose affection you keep in the way of ordered charity. With constancy that cannot waver it advances towards you, and by the help of your grace it so prospers in its progress that it will not give up until you make it perfect. With that wealth of your sweetness that you hide for the fearful[62] you are wont to crown the souls who hope, especially those whose works shine before the children of men to your glory, O Father in heaven.[63] These are the souls who love you. When I see such and do not find myself among them, I weary of my life. Their wisdom comes not from the spirit of this world, nor from the prudence of this present age. Being devoid of learning, they have entered into the power of the Lord[64] and, being poor in spirit,[65] they are mindful only of your righteousness. Wherefore you have taught them, that in their life and conduct they may show forth your wondrous works.[66] These are your simple servants, with whom you are wont to talk familiarly.[67] In coming to you they do not put their trust in the chariots of their own cleverness, nor in the horses of their own strength, but only in the name of the Lord.[68]

15. Thus with your wisdom sweetly ordering all things for them[69] they come by a short road and lightly laden to their appointed end, where chariots and horsemen fail. They do not form pictures of

---

61. Gen 1:27.
64. Ps 70:15f.
67. Prov 3:32.

62. Ps 30:20.
65. Mt 5:3.
68. Ps 19:8.

63. Mt 5:16.
66. Ps 70:17.
69. Wis 8:1.

your love, nor do they compare it to their own by any subtle reasoning; rather, your love itself, finding in them simple material on which to work, so forms them and conforms them to itself in both affection and effect, that, besides what is hidden within[70]—namely, the glory and riches of a good conscience[71]—the inner light is reflected in their outward appearance, and that not by deliberate effort but by a certain connaturality. And so much is this the case, that the charm and the simplicity of their expression and bearing provoke love of you; indeed the very sight of them sometimes moves even barbarous and boorish souls to love you.[72] In such people nature indeed returns to the fountain whence it sprang. Having no human teacher, they are ready to be taught by God,[73] and when, with the help of the Spirit who has compassion on their infirmity,[74] their spirits enter into the divine movement and their senses are controlled by a certain spiritual discipline, a certain spirituality appears even in their bodies, and their faces acquire an appearance that is more than human, having a singular and very special grace. Through devotion to good practices their flesh that is sown in corruption begins even now to rise again to glory;[75] so that heart and flesh together may rejoice in the living God,[76] and where the soul thirsts after you the flesh also may thirst in O how many ways![77] For the blessed meek possess the earth of their own body;[78] which earth, made fruitful by the faithful practice of spiritual exercises, even though it has been left to go fallow, bears fruit of itself in fastings, in watchings, in labors, being ready for every good work[79] without contradiction of sloth.

16. When I see these people, I am wholly drawn to the love of your love, which effects this in them. Your love in them I grasp by

---

70. Song 4:1, 3.   71. Ps 111:3.

72. Cf. *On the Nature and Dignity of Love*, n. 43 (Cistercian Fathers Series 15).

73. Jn 6:45.   74. Rom 8:26.   75. 1 Cor 15:42f.

76. Ps 83:3.   77. Ps 62:2.

78. Mt 5:4. William shares with Bernard of Clairvaux this interpretation of the earth as being the man's own body. See St Bernard's *First Sermon for the Feast of All Saints*, n. 9 (Cistercian Fathers Series 22).

79. Tit 3:1.

a certain sure experience known to those who love. I love them, therefore, because they love you. And I love them much, even as I love in them the love with which you are loved. And if I love them in this way, so that I love nothing except you in them and in their natural affection[80] which is full of you and never love my own affection unless I find myself attracted to you, what then do I love save you in those whom I love in you, and in myself whom I desire to love in you alone? The answer is, surely, nothing. For if I perceive myself to love them and myself in any other way, I hate myself more than I love myself in this respect.

17. So, then, I find you in my love, O Lord, but O that I might always find you there! For since love is not love unless it loves, and yet the will for you is always vehement in me—that is to say, your love that urges me to you, why, then, are my affections not always taken up with you? Is love one thing, and the feeling of love another? As I see it, love is a natural thing, but to love you belongs to grace; the feeling of love is a manifestation of grace, and of that the Apostle says: "To each one is given the manifestation of the Spirit to profit withal."[81] For so long as "the body that is subject to corruption weighs down the soul, and the earthly habitation presses down the mind that muses upon many things,"[82] the soul is bound to experience vicissitudes, however much it loves; and, if the affection did not comfort it at one extreme and restrain it in the other, it would inevitably come to a ruin, from which no further advance would ever raise it.

18. In the soul of your poor servant, therefore, Lord, your love is always present; but it is hidden like the fire in the ashes till the Holy Spirit, who blows where he wills,[83] is pleased to manifest it profitably the way and to the extent he wishes. Come, therefore, come, O holy Love; come, O sacred Fire! Burn up the concupiscences of our reins and our hearts.[84] Hide your thoughts as you will, to furnish more abundantly the rule of humility for your revealing flame.

---

80. The Mazarine ends here. For the rest it is necessary to depend exclusively on the Migne edition.

81. 1 Cor 12:7.   82. Wis 9:15.   83. Jn 3:8.   84. Ps 25:2.

Manifest them when you will, to manifest the glory of a good conscience and the riches it has in its house.[85] Manifest those riches, Lord, to make me zealous to keep them; hide them from me, lest I be led rashly to squander them, until such time as he who has begun the good work shall also perfect it,[86] he who lives and reigns through all the ages of ages.

85. Ps 111:3.   86. Phil 1:6.

MEDITATION THIRTEEN

INTRODUCTION

THE MOVING DIALOGUE which we have come to call *Meditation Thirteen* was transcribed towards the end of the twelfth century, perhaps a little later, on two pages which had been left empty between William's *Mirror of Faith* and *Enigma of Faith*[1] in Ms. 114 of Charleville.[2] It was written by a hand different from that of the rest of the manuscript and undoubtedly after the volume had been put together.[3] The writing, which is not always very clear, is rather irregular. Besides the contemporary abbreviations there are many others which are not common. The spaces between the lines vary, the margins are unequal, and the pages have not been prepared to receive a text. The text on the second page has been squeezed together and looks like it was written hurriedly. It seems the copyist was pressed for time and feared that he would not have enough space. In a word there is nothing here which resembles the impeccable method and regularity of official copies. This without doubt then was inserted as an afterthought and probably rather late.

1. *The Works of William of St Thierry*, vol. 3 (Cistercian Fathers Series 9).
2. Ff. 77 verso—78 recto.
3. Ms. 114 of Charleville (twelfth-century coming from Signy) is the only collection of the works of William which has come down to us. It contains: 1. an extract of a personal commentary on the Song of Songs; 2. *The Golden Epistle to the Carthusians of Mont-Dieu*; 3. *The Mirror of Faith*; 4. *Meditation Thirteen*; 5. *The Ænigma of Faith*; 6. *The Exposition on the Song of Songs*.

Until recently no one thought to try to identify the text. Fooled by the title: *Excerpts from the Meditations of Dom William*, great scholars like Dom Wilmart, and editors like Mlle. Davy saw there only "a brief extract" or "an insignificant extract" from the Meditations of Abbot William.[4] Our surprise then was the greater in discovering an integral piece, a thirteenth *Meditation* of a character more intimate than the first twelve, very moving, and of very great interest in regard to the life history of its author. It is, in fact, possible for us to situate it with exactitude in the life of William. Its value in view of this is considerably augmented.

By internal criticism alone we are already able to discover certain indications as to the circumstances of its composition.

The author had heard the pressing appeal of God and had responded to it generously, perhaps too generously. He had fled into the "desert" (*desertum* in the twelfth century was either Chartreuse or Cîteaux) embracing the yoke of the Lord and choosing the narrow way, which he had seen chosen by others, his fathers, his models; in a word, he had become a religious in an austere order. He expected to find in his new *conversatio* the peace of a life wholly given to God, the sweetness, the consolation promised to the strong, to the courageous, to those who did not baulk against the burden of obedience and of absolute detachment; but in place of that, he found only pain and weariness. His flesh was suffering violence. The weakness of his sick body, his debility, his exhaustion, played against his spirit, soon crushed and failing. In the midst of this trial, the author felt himself alone, abandoned by God and man. He did not know to whom he could turn, or in any case he did not understand at the moment, he did not see the relationship between his good will and the misery which crushed him. The gift which he had made of himself appeared to him to be poorly recompensed and he complained to the Lord.

All this is, indeed, clear. And a passage of the *Vita* puts it into context for us:

4. See D. Wilmart, "La Série et la date des ouvrages de Guillaume de St-Thierry" in *Revue Mabillon*, 16 (1924), p. 167, note 3; and M. M. Davy, *Meditativae Orationes* (Paris: Vrin, 1934), p. 33.

Attracted by the kind of unmitigated life which one professed to live in the Order of Cîteaux, and inflamed by a desire for solitude and spiritual repose, Dom William abandoned the burden and the honors of his prelacy to receive the holy habit of poverty at Signy. Sure of himself, full of confidence in his vocation, he served God in holiness and justice to the best of his ability.[5]

However, he had not taken into account his own body and the weakness of his nature:

> Taken away from his habitual way of doing things and weakened by a diet which was insufficient he quickly began to ask himself if he had not presumed too much on his own forces and if he could live his new way of life.[6]

The text goes on to relate the trial of which we have spoken and the temptation to turn back:

> At that time he suffered from this temptation and he could not hide what he was bearing, but to one of the monks who was his friend, the one who had been his Prior at the Abbey of St Thierry and had followed him into the desert, he confessed his fault. This monk, as an admiring disciple, was amazed and could hardly believe it and sought to comfort his master. . . . The master heard the comforting words but he did not experience any relief because his ways were not human ways nor did it belong to any man to direct his steps. Realizing this, he begged the Lord in devout prayers that what was not possible to him, humanly speaking, God's grace might make possible.[7]

This account from the *Vita* is in perfect harmony with that which we learned in this *Meditation* concerning its author. This dialogue can only be one of those prayers by which William implored the help of heaven against his weakness and the deficiencies of his nature.[8] More suggestive still is the solution of the incident as it is recounted in the *Vita:*

---

5. *Vita Antiqua* (anonymous) ms. Paris B. N. lat. 11782, ff. 340f. in *Mélanges Godefroid Kurth*, vol. 1 (Liège, 1908), p. 90.

6. *Ibid.* p. 91.   7. *Ibid.* p. 91f.

8. Compare the *quod minus habebat* of the *Vita* with the *quod minus potes* of this *Meditation*.

And so it was done. He manifestly experienced the effect of divine power, and his temptation entirely vanished. The yoke of the Lord was again sweet and the burden light. . . . The true Elijah sprinkling the meal experienced a greater sweetness in the plain food of the deserts and the rough cloth of his habit than he used to experience in furs and fishes.[9]

William did not ask for so much, but that sweet yoke harks back to the dialogue of the *Meditation*.

In summary, the *Vita* gives us a guarantee of the authenticity of the *Meditation Thirteen* as is found in the Charleville Manuscripts. After the death of William, a religious of Signy discovered this dialogue among the papers of the man of God, quite possibly joined to the original *Meditations* which had already been published, or perhaps among other prayers or written meditations which were left unedited. This is the simplest explanation for the insertion of this very intimate page into a tome of the works of the former abbot and given the generic title *Extracts from the Meditations of Dom William*. It is quite easy to establish the similarities between this *Meditation* and one or other of the other twelve *Meditations*. The *Fourth Meditation* seems to also be concerned with the trial of the author at Signy.[10] It also brings us through to the victory as does the *Vita* and the same expressions, figures, terms of *Meditation Thirteen* are found there also.[11] The *Eleventh Meditation* is even more suggestive.[12] But the citation from Mark 14:8, apropos to the sinful woman who did what she could, is found also in the *Fifth Meditation*, as well as in the *Golden Epistle*.[13] The text of Isaiah (46:4) is found also in the *First Meditation*.[14] In regard to the theme of Christ compare what we have here with *Meditations Ten* and *Eleven*.[15]

These points of contact, this community of atmosphere, justify in a certain way the title given by the scribe to this *Meditation* of

---

9. *Vita antiqua*, p. 92.

10. See above, pp. 111f.

11. See above, pp. 112f.

12. See above, pp. 157f.

13. See above, p. 123; also *The Golden Epistle*, Pref.

14. See above, p. 89.

15. See above, pp. 154f, pp. 157ff.

William's and establish another argument in favor of the authenticity of this wonderful little treatise.[16]

One should not let himself be deceived by the lack of style here, even though ordinarily William's is more flowing and more correct. We are far from the period of rich maturity which will produce the *Golden Epistle* or the long developments in the *Exposition on the Song of Songs*. The relative imperfection is sufficiently explained by the nature of his *Meditation* and the circumstances of its composition. It is quite moving even with its lack of polish. It flows from a heart which is weighed down and it is spread over the paper with the flight of the pen without any concern to create style, or even simply to write. There is here something spontaneous, something lived, without preparation or retouches. In the mind of William, this intimate dialogue with God was not destined to leave the *sacrarium* of his personal notes and papers. But the man who inserted this historic prayer among the works of William was certainly well inspired.

J. M. Déchanet OSB

16. We can add that entire pages of *The Golden Epistle* (e.g., nn. 18f.; n. 32) are a reply to the question of this Meditation: "How to rule and guard it (the body) while I remain alive, that I may yield to none of its irrational desires, and yet refuse it nothing that it really needs." (Below, pp. 187f.).

MEDITATION THIRTEEN

LORD, YOU HAVE LED ME ASTRAY, and I have followed your leading; you were the stronger, and you have prevailed.[1] I heard you say: "Come unto me, all you who labor and are heavy laden, and I will refresh you."[2] I came to you, I trusted in your word, and in what way have you refreshed me? I was not laboring before, but I am laboring now and ready to drop with the toil! I was not burdened formerly, but now I am worn out beneath my load. You also said: "My yoke is pleasant and my burden light."[3] Where is that pleasantness? Where is that lightness? Already I grow weary of the yoke, already I am fainting beneath the burden. I have looked all round, and there is no one to help me; and I have sought, but there is nobody to give me aid.[4] Lord, what does this mean? Have mercy on me, for I am weak.[5] Where are your mercies of old?[6] Our fathers, who preceded us along this road, did they possess the earth by their own sword? Was it their own arm that saved them?[7] Most surely it was not; it was your arm and the light of your countenance.[8] Why was that so? Because they were found pleasing in your sight.[9] O you who command the saving of Jacob, you are my king and God.[10] What, then, is it in me

---

1. Jer 20:7.
2. Mt 11:28.
3. Mt 11:30.
4. Is 63:5; Ps 106:12.
5. Ps 6:3.
6. Ps 88:50.
7. Ps 43:2ff.
8. *Ibid.*
9. *Ibid.*
10. Ps 43:5.

that has displeased you, Lord? Why do you not judge your servant?
You said, with reference to the homage of the sinful woman: "She
has done what she could."[11] Have I not also done all that I could?
Indeed it seems to me that I have done more than I thought I had
the power to do!

2. *The Lord:* My son, do not despise your father's chastening; do
not grow weary when you are reproved by him;[12] for "whom the
Lord loves he chastens and scourges every son whom he receives."[13]
Indeed what son is there whom his father does not correct? If you
are beyond chastening, you are a bastard, not a son.[14] I have not led
you astray, my son; I have led you sweetly on until now. That
which was said to you, that which was cried to you: "Come unto
me," has been cried aloud to all; but all do not receive the grace to
come.[15] To you it has been given so to do in preference to many
great ones who are rich in their own eyes. Have I committed sin in
doing good to you? You complain that I do not refresh you. If I had
not refreshed you, you would have fainted away. You groan
beneath my yoke and weary of my burden. The thing that makes
the sweetness of my yoke, the lightness of my burden, is charity. If
you had charity, then you would feel that sweetness. Your flesh
would not labor, if it loved you;[16] or, if it did, charity would
mitigate the toil. You cannot bear my burden and my yoke alone;
but if you have charity along with you to share the yoke and the
burden you will be surprised to find how sweet they are.

3. *Response:* Lord, that is what I said. I have done what I could.
The thing that seems to have been given into my own power,
namely, my wretched body and my feeble limbs, I have handed over

---

11. Mk 14:8. William employs this same text in *Meditation Five*, n. 10,
above, p. 123; and in the Preface of the *Golden Epistle*.

12. Prov 3:11; Heb 12:5.   13. Heb 12:6.

14. Heb 12:7ff.   15. Cf. Mt 20:16; 22:14.

16. "If it loved you." The sense is if the flesh sought less its own satisfaction
and served more the purposes of the spirit. This is an allusion to the order of
charity which holds an important place in the ascesis of William of St Thierry.
See e.g. the *Exposition on the Song of Songs*, n. 128; Hart trans., *The Works of
William of St. Thierry*, vol. 2 (Cistercian Fathers Series 6), pp. 102f.

to your service. Had it been also in my power to have charity, I should have reached perfection long ago. If you do not bestow it then I have not got it; and if I may not have it, I cannot go on. You know, you see how little I can do. Take of that little whatever you will, and give me that full and perfect charity.

4. *The Lord:* Am I then to supply your deficiencies and also give you the charity for which you ask? But, my son, you must accept my chastening.[17] There is no going except by the Way. If you do not forsake this road, then you will reach your goal. I myself go before you,[18] and you must follow as you see me go before. I endured and labored and you must labor too. I suffered many things, it behoves you too to suffer some. Obedience is the way to charity, and you will get there if you keep to it. But you must recognize how great a thing is charity, and worthy to be bought at a high price. For God is charity;[19] when you reach that you will labor no more.

5. *Response:* Lord, my frame which you have made is not hidden from you, nor is my substance in the depths of earth. Your eyes have seen my imperfection.[20] I dare not ask to be relieved of labor, nor do I want to do so; but in the meantime, while I have not got charity, who is to bear the toil along with me?

6. *The Lord:* I have made, and I will bear.[21] But, if you have been ungrateful for the gifts that you have received already, you will be judged unworthy to receive greater ones. You have already been given a measure of charity; but you either do not know it, or are ungrateful for it. Charity belongs to wisdom, and the beginning of wisdom is the fear of the Lord.[22] The fear of God has already led you up to this present point; already it has put you in this place whence, if the end should find you there, you will go forth in safety. It has led you thus far, it has put you here, it is keeping you

---

17. Song 2:12.   18. Cf. Ex 13:21; Deut 1:33; Josh 3:3.

19. 1 Jn 4:16.   20. Ps 138:15f.

21. Is 46:4. William has already quoted this in the opening lines of the *First Meditation*; see above, p. 89.

22. Prov 1:7.

here. Have you then made so little progress? Is it so little that you have hitherto received?

7. *Response:* Truly, Lord, you are become our refuge;[23] I have fled to you, teach me your will[24] and make me do it. You have had compassion on the people that followed you into the wilderness. You have had pity and have provided food, lest they faint by the way.[25] I have begun to follow you, my leader, into the wilderness; I have vowed and I am determined to keep the judgments of your righteousness.[26] By your grace I will not forsake you; I will not withdraw myself from you until either I come to the goal whither you have begun to bring me, or I fall in my tracks as you yourself fell, if it is possible to fall following you. For I know that, even if the body is weak and even if the spirit sometimes wearies, I shall not fail if I do not forsake you, but shall make progress by means of my infirmities,[27] provided you do not forsake me by depriving me of patience. Have mercy on me, Lord; look on my low estate and poverty.[28] Help me and carry me, weak and feeble as I am in both mind and body. Inspire those who love you, your servants and your sons, to help me and to carry me, and out of my wretchedness to gain the rewards of their patience and their pity. I am yours: O save me.[29] Into your hands I commend my spirit.[30] Teach it and rule it, encourage, comfort and enlighten it. Give me wisdom that sits upon your throne, that she may be with me and may labor with me, that I may know at all times what is acceptable in your sight.[31] But do not reject me from the number of your children, for I am your servant, and your servants' servant too.[32]

8. As to my body, Lord, I do not know what to ask; you know what is good for me concerning it. If it so please you, let it be strong and healthy; and equally, if you so will, let it be weak and sick. And when it is your will that it should die, then let it die, provided only that the spirit finds salvation in your day. For this one

23. Ps 89:1.

24. Ps 142:9f.

25. Mt 15:32.

26. Ps 118:106.

27. Cf. 2 Cor 12:9.

28. Song 9:14.

29. Ps 118:94.

30. Ps 30:6; Lk 23:46.

31. Wis 9:4, 10.

32. Wis 9:4f.

thing only do I implore your mercy in regard to my body—
namely, that you would teach me how to rule and guard it, while I
remain alive, that I may yield to none of its irrational desires, and yet
refuse it nothing that it really needs.

9. The end of the law is charity,[33] and that is the end of my prayer.
O you who have willed to be called charity, give me charity, that
I may love you more than I love myself, not caring at all what I do
with myself, so long as I am doing what is pleasing in your sight.
Grant me, O Father—though I dare not always call myself your
child—grant me at least to be your faithful little servant and the
sheep of your pasture. Speak to your servant's heart sometimes, O
Lord, so that your consolations may give joy to my soul.[34] And
teach me to speak to you often in prayer. Take to yourself all my
poverty and need, O Lord, my God and Father. Have pity on my
weakness, you who are my strength.[35] And may it be to your great
glory that my feebleness continues to serve you. Amen.

---

33. 1 Tim 1:5.   34. Ps 93:19   35. Ps 117:14.

SELECTED BIBLIOGRAPHY

The translations of the treatise, *On Contemplating God*, and of the *Prayer*, are based on the critical Latin text established by Dom Jacques Hourlier and published in Sources Chrétiennes 61 (Paris, 1959). For the *Meditations* (1–12) M. M. Davy's edition of Mazarine 776 (Paris 1934) was compared with that of Robert Thomas, Pain de Cîteaux 21-22 (Chambarland, 1964). In some instances, the latter prefers readings found in the Migne edition (PL 180:205–248), which depends on some other unknown manuscript source through the edition of Tissier (Bonne-Fontaine, 1669). The translation usually follows him in this. Some correctives were also brought to the text by Dom Hourlier. The translation of *Meditation Thirteen* is based on the edition of Charleville 114 published by Dom J. M. Déchanet, in *Collectanea O.C.R.*, 7 (1940), pp. 2–12 and reproduced as an appendix in his book, *Guillaume de Saint-Thierry: L'Homme et son Oeuvre* (Bruges, 1942; trans. Cistercian Studies Series 10).

In the treatise, *On Contemplating God*, the paragraph numbers found in the critical edition have been retained. For the *Meditations* we have adopted those found in the edition of Robert Thomas.

Since 1959 when the critical Latin texts were published there has been a revival of interest in William of St Thierry. Some of the new studies devoted to him serve to complement our knowledge of these treatises, but they do not modify it appreciably. The present edition then offers a succinct bibliography. To this can be added the works devoted to other twelfth-century authors, especially to Bernard. One can also make use of various other articles of the *Dictionnaire de Spiritualité*, such as contemplation, unlikeness, divinization, *examinatio*, and ecstasy.

Brooke, O., "The Speculative Development of the Trinitarian Theology of William of Saint Thierry in the *Aenigma Fidei*," in *R.T.A.M.*, 27 (1960), pp. 193–211, 28 (1961), pp. 26–58.

"The Trinitarian Aspect of the Ascent of the Soul to God in the Theology of William of Saint Thierry" in *R.T.A.M.*, 26 (1959), pp. 85–127.

Elder, E. Rozanne, "The Way of Ascent: the Meaning of Love in the Thought of William of Saint-Thierry" in *Studies in Medieval Culture*, I, ed. J. R. Sommerfeldt (Western Michigan University, ser. VII, no. 2) 1964, pp. 39–47.

Fiske, A., "William of St. Thierry and Friendship" in *Cîteaux*, 12 (1961), pp. 5–27.

Koehler, T., "Thème et Vocabulaire de la 'Fruition divine' chez Guillaume de Saint-Thierry" in *R.A.M.*, 40 (1964), pp. 139–160.

Magrassi, Mariano, *Teologia e Storia nel Pensiero di Ruperto di Deutz* (Rome: Pontificia Universita de Propaganda Fide, 1959).

Pellegrino, M., "Tracce de Saint Agostino nel Contemplando" in *Rev. des Études Augustiniennes*, 9 (1963), p. 103.

Ruello, F., in the *Rev. de l'Histoire des Religions*, 161 (1962), pp. 85–89, reviews the critical ed. (Sources Chrétiennes 61) and insists on the notion of salvation contained in William.

Ryan, P., "The Witness of William of St Thierry to the Spirit and Aims of the Early Cistercians" in *The Cistercian Spirit*, ed., M. B. Pennington, Cistercian Studies Series 3, 1969, pp. 224–253.

Thomas, R., "Notre Entrée dans la Vie Trinitaire d'après Guillaume de Saint-Thierry" in *Collectanea O.C.R.*, 24 (1962), pp. 209–224; 338–349.

Walsh, J., "William of Saint-Thierry and Spiritual Meanings" in *R.A.M.*, 35 (1959), pp. 27–42.

ANALYTIC INDEX

Numbers refer to paragraphs in the texts; in the case of Med the number before the colon refers to the *Meditation* in which the paragraph can be found. The following abbreviations are used: CG=*On Contemplating God;* Med= *Meditations;* P=*Prayer.*

Laus tibi, Christe

CISTERCIAN STUDIES SERIES

Under the direction of the same Board of Editors as the CISTERCIAN FATHERS SERIES, the CISTERCIAN STUDIES SERIES seeks to make available to the English-speaking world significant studies produced in other languages, as well as various monastic texts and studies of perennial value, with a view to placing the Cistercian Fathers in their full historical context and bringing out their present-day relevance.

CS1 Thomas Merton: *The Climate of Monastic Prayer*
     Introduction: Douglas V Steere

CS2 Amédée Hallier, *The Monastic Theology of Aelred of Rievaulx: An Experiential Theology*
     Introduction: Thomas Merton

CS3 *The Cistercian Spirit: A Symposium*
     In Memory of Thomas Merton (Fr Louis ocso)

CS4 Evagrius Ponticus: *The Praktikos and 153 Chapters on Prayer*

Cistercian Publications   Spencer   Massachusetts   01562

Irish University Press   Shannon   Ireland